Caique Pai

Caiques as pets.

Caique Keeping, Care, Pros and Cons, Housing, Diet and Health.

by

Roger Rodendale

Table of Contents

Introduction

For anyone who is looking for an entertaining and fun loving pet, a Caique parrot is the perfect option. Although these birds are not recommended for first time bird owners, they can be a lot of fun if you are able to find the right assistance to raise your bird.

Some of the most common sights with the Caique parrot is the bird rolling on his back, being comfortable when rolled over, hopping all over the house and just being his comical self.

These birds come with strong personalities and therefore you need to be sure that they are well socialized. For the most part, they will be friendly with everyone in your household and will even form strong bonds with the family. Although they will form one strong bond with one member of the family, they will recognize the rest as their flock.

Caique parrots are very intelligent which means that you will be able to get the birds to learn several tricks. This can be a great way to spend some quality time with your bird. These extremely active birds are very playful and can become that big bundle of energy that everyone simply loves.

Now the issue with these birds is that they need to be handled very well. In the hands of someone with less knowledge about the bird, they can become very noisy. They are inherently stubborn which means that you need to provide them with a strong routine and some rigid boundaries to keep them well behaved. They also need to be handled well to ensure that they do not become too nippy.

This book will give you all the information that you need with respect to raising your Caique parrots right. These birds are medium sized and will demand everything that a medium sized parrot requires. That includes the supplies, the housing, diet and just about everything.

This book will break down these medium sized bird requirements for you so that you know exactly what to give your bird. The book also helps you understand general care requirements such as housing the bird, introducing them to family pets, giving them a nutritious diet and even grooming them.

Details about training the bird and handling them correctly have been included so that you can form a strong relationship with your beloved pet.

The intention of the book is to become your guide to bringing Caique parrots home as pets. From choosing the right bird to making the transition into your home simple and caring for the bird, this book covers everything.

Since the book is a compilation of real life accounts from Caique owners, you can be certain that all the methods have been tried to give you success with raising your bird.

These tips are also very easy to understand and are extremely practical. It is a good idea that you read the book thoroughly, understand the demands of a Caique parrot and then bring one home with all the right information in place.

Chapter 1: Knowing Caiques

The Caique parrot is popularly known as the clown of the parrot world. The funny demeanor of the bird that is coupled with the awkward antics make them the most entertaining companions that you can bring home.

To begin with, most new owners find it hard to pronounce the name of the species. So to break it down, it is usually pronounced as "Kigh-eek" or "kah-eek". If you are going to own a bird, you must know how to say the name!

Of course, these birds are not great talkers. They are vocal but cannot imitate human language very well. They may pick up a few words such as "hello" but most often than not, these birds will not learn to talk. So, if you want a parrot whose mimicry skills you can show off, the Caique is not your best bet.

In most cases, the Caiques that do learn to talk are the single pets. They are likely to learn words and to context. Their talking voice is extremely low and they will, as mentioned above, learn a word or two. But, the noteworthy thing about that is that they will use the word in context quite well. So they will greet you with a hello and will probably say goodbye when you leave.

But, these birds have so much personality that you simply cannot cross out the amazing things about being a Caique owner. They will learn to whistle almost to perfection. They will even carry a tune when you whistle along with them.

They may not really speak but they can learn several tricks, as they are highly intelligent creatures. These training sessions also double as great playtime with your beloved parrot. These birds are active and will pick up skills quite easily.

As for the physical appearance, the most striking thing about Caiques is their plumage. They are brightly colored in shades of yellow and green. These are medium sized birds. The body is short and stocky. This appearance is enhanced by the square tail that seems to make the body look even shorter.

They weigh between 150-170 grams. The average life span of a Caique is 40 years. That brings us to another very important point about owning Caiques or any other parrot. These birds are probably going to be passed on from one generation to the other. In any case, you must picture your life 40 years from now and know if you can still manage to have a Caique as a pet. They need to have a lot of mental stimulation. It is not just about feeding and keeping the surroundings of your bird clean. It is a relationship that you must be very consistent with.

There are two species of Caiques that have gained popularity among pet owners. These are the white bellied Caique and the black headed Caique. We will discuss in detail about each species and its sub species in the following section.

1.Caique species and sub-species

Caiques are parrots that hail from South America. Parrots from this region are known as "New World Parrots". One feature that distinguishes the Caique from all the other parrots from this region is the white breast.

These birds are sexually monomorphic. This means that the male and female birds look exactly the same and it is not possible to distinguish them visually.

There are two main species of these birds which are the White bellied Caique and the Black headed Caique. There are five sub species under them. We will learn about them in more detail in this section.

White bellied Caiques

These birds are usually found in the Southern part of the River Amazon in Brazil. Their range also extends to Peru, Ecuador and Bolivia. These birds are usually seen in the forest canopies. Their preferred habitat is the coastal forest area. You will normally see these birds in pairs, in small flocks or in groups of families. They are usually located by their screeching noise, which is persistent almost all day long.

The majority of the time in a Caique's day is dedicated to feeding on fruits, seeds and berries. They will forage on the treetops to find their food.

7

There are three sub species under the While bellied Caiques:

Green thigh white belly
This is one of the main races of the white bellied Caique. However, not many have made their way into captivity, especially in the United States. The name comes from the green plumes that cover the thigh region of the bird. These birds are normally seen in the Amazon region in Brazil.

They are seen in the seasonally flooded areas in the forest and the lowlands in the tropical and humid regions.

Yellow thigh white belly
This is the most commonly seen white belly sub species. In many cases, the white bellied Caiques are synonymous with the yellow thigh white bellied. You can refer to the same bird with both names although the yellow thigh is a sub species of the white bellied Caique.

Yellow tailed white belly
This sub species is considered to be the palest in terms of coloration. This sub species is not prevalent in the United States. In fact, in comparison to the other two sub species, their geographical range is also much smaller. These birds are currently limited only to Europe. These birds are known for their characteristic pink feet. They are also seen in the southern part of Brazil that is drained by the Amazon River. The habitat is similar to the green thigh parrot.

There are some characteristics that are similar in all the white bellied Caiques. For instance, the breast is fluffy and white. This type of plumage extends to the abdomen of the bird. The crown, the nape, the upper ear coverts and the hind neck are bright orange in color. The sides of the head, the cheeks and the throat are bright yellow in color. As for the tail, the rump, under tail coverts and the back, the coloration is usually bright green except for the yellow tailed Caique. The primary coverts and the primaries are a striking violet blue with a dark green edge. The beak in the birds is horn colored. The feet and the legs range from grey to pink in color. In adults the iris is usually orange or dark red in color.

In case of the immature white bellied Caique, the coloration on the feathers is dull in comparison to the adults. You can identify them by the yellow wash on the abdomen. They will also have dark feathers on the head. These dark feathers are interspersed with orange feathers making the plumage look brindled. In some cases, it will seem like a solid dark colored crown.

In most cases, the clutch will consist of chicks that are of the same color. However, there are chances that there are dark and light colored chicks in one single clutch. In the first molt, the dark feathers will be replaced with orange when the bird is about one year old.

If there are any remaining dark feathers, they will be shed in the successive molting seasons. Eventually, the head will appear bright orange in color. The darker the plumes when they are chicks, the brighter the orange coloration will be.

Black headed Caiques
In the northern region of the Amazon River in Colombia, Brazil, French Guiana, Venezuela, Guyana and Surinam, you will find the second most popular species of Caiques, which is the black headed Caique. These birds are seen in the edges of the forests, the high forests and even the woodlands in the savannahs. These parrots are known for being extremely noisy.

They will be seen in flocks of up to 30 or in small family groups. They will spend most of their time perched on trees and feeding on nuts, berries, seeds and fruits. If they are disturbed these birds will fly away instantly making a loud screeching sound.

One subspecies of the black headed Caique *'Poinite Melanocephalamelanocephalais'*, the most well-known one. The abdomen and the breast of this bird have fluffy white feathers. The crown, the nape and the forehead are black in color. The throat and cheeks are yellow and the have a small green streak just below the eye in the front part of the head.

The neck of the bird is orange. The back, the tail and the wings are green in color while the thighs are orange in color. The feet are colored from grey to black. The beak is usually black and the iris is a dark red color in case of the adults.

You have another subspecies which is also called the *Pointes Melanocephalapallida.* These birds are distinct because all the orange feathers are replaced by yellow ones. It is believed that a hybrid between birds in captivity and wild birds is the reason for the color variation that you see in these birds.

In case of the immature black headed Caiques, the plumage is duller and they also have a very heavy yellow-orange wash on the abdomen and breast. The beak is grey in color and the eyes are dark in case of the juvenile birds.

2.Taxonomy of Caiques

Caiques are classified under the genus *Poinites.* Initially, it was believed that these birds had only two species, namely the white bellied and the black headed Caiques. However, there were a total of five sub species that were discovered over the years.

These birds were often allied with South American parakeets and conures. However the study of the nuclear DNA and the mitochondria of the bird has found that the birds under the genus *Poinites*are are similar to the genus *Deroptyus,* which consists of birds like the red fan parrot.

The species and subspecies of the Caique parrots are classified as follows:

* Green thigh white belly: *Poinitesleucogasterleucogaster*
* Yellow thigh white belly: *Poinitesleucogasterxanthomeria*
* Yellow tail white belly: *Poinitesleucogaster*xanthurus
* Black headed: *Poinitesmelanocephalamelanocephala*
* Black headed hybrid: *Poinitesmelanocephalapallida*

The general classification of the Caique parrot is as follows:
Kingdom: *Animalia*
Phylum: *Chordata*
Class: *Aves*
Order: *Pssittaciformes*
Superfamily: *Psittacoidea*
Family: *Psittacidae*
Sub Family: *Arinae*
Genus*: Poinites*

10

Knowing these details helps you understand the birds that are similar in anatomy and classification to your pet. That will help you learn more about the care, the requirements, the general misconceptions and other details by comparison. That way your source of information is never very limited.

3.Natural History of Caiques

In the natural setting, these birds are usually found in the edge of forests and also in secondary growth areas. They are most often seen in the higher areas of the forest canopy where they spend most of their time foraging. In some cases, the birds are also seen in the lower areas of the forest edges.

One unique feature of Caiques is that they take turns to guard the flock, especially when they are feeding. Commonly, at least two birds will act as sentries or guards to the flock when they are eating. These birds are omnivorous. A majority of the diet consists of pulp, fruits, flowers and seeds. Insects are eaten seldom in the wild and most often when these birds are kept in captivity. This depends on the diet that you decide to put your bird on in consultation with your avian vet.

Breeding season varies depending upon the location of the birds and the species of Caiques in question. However, on an average, the breeding season lasts from October to May. These birds are known to breed several times each year. These birds will nest in the higher parts of the canopy. They will build their nests in the cavities of the trees that they are perched on.

Caiques are known to be communal roosters. This is a very common trait of the new world parrots. This means that in the presence of certain external signs, these birds will roost in large flocks. Then, when the sign disappears, the flock will disperse and the birds will return to preferred areas of the habitat, mostly the spots where they have made their nests. These signs could include nightfall, changes in the weather or in some cases, high tides. Most of the Caique birds will be seen in large flocks whose numbers will range from 10 to about 30.

This does not imply that they will observe cooperative roosting. The difference between the two types of roosting is that in communal roosting, you will not see any chicks. These chicks are restricted to the nesting areas that parents will return to after the signs disappear.

What is noteworthy in the natural habitat of Caiques is the very obvious distinction between the habitats of the two species. The white bellied Caiques are seen in the southern part of the Amazon River in forests that are humid and also in the wooded areas. Their range extends from Brazil and Bolivia to Peru.

There are several protected areas in the natural range of the white bellied Caiques, as they are considered endangered species. Some of the most popular protected areas include the Tambopata-Candamo in Peru, Manu National Park in Peru, the Amazonia national Park in Brazil and the Madidi National Park in Bolivia.

As for the black headed Caiques, you will see them in the northern part of River Amazon and in the western part of the Ucayali River. Their range extends from North Brazil, Bolovia, Ecuador, Colombia, Bolivia, Guyana, French Guyana, and Venezuela to Peru. These birds also inhabit some protected areas in the natural range that they are seen in.

Caiques will seldom be seen outside their range and habitat. This is because these birds lack the ability to fly over long distances as a flock. This is also a major reason for the sharp distinction in the habitats of the two species of Caiques.

4.Personality of the Caique

This is the most important thing for a potential Caique owner to be aware of. These birds are striking in their physical appearance and that may motivate several bird lovers to have them at home as pets.

However, what matters more is whether you can really handle the personality of the bird. They are very active birds that are known to be quite comical as well. These birds know no fear. Many Caique owners describe their birds as extremely determined creatures. If the bird wants something, he will do everything in his ability to get it. Even pushing them away, some owners say, does not work as they will run back to the object.

Caiques are described as beaky birds, which means that they like to nip. That is why hand raising them is very important. If you ask a Caique owner, he will tell you that the favorite part of the hand that they like to bite is the skin between two fingers. That, dear reader, is the most sensitive part of the hand. Therefore, most owners will find this personality trait rather inconvenient and annoying.

In most cases, this "beakiness" is not the result of any anger or irritation. Caiques are curious birds and love to explore the area around them. Of course, they will do this with their beaks and in the bargain, may end up hurting you or someone in your family. However it is possible to distract the bird with wooden toys or perches when you feel like the biting is getting a little rough.

The temperament of the bird is another thing that you need to know about. For the most part, these birds are fun loving, confident and happy. But, they can get irked by several things. For instance, try to take something away from your bird and you will unleash his temper. When they are angry, Caiques tend to be very loud and will let out a loud squeal. Some of them will even try to bite your hand.

These birds are stubborn. That is one more personality quirk that you need to be familiar with. If you bring a Caique home and begin training them, there may be some commands that they will just ignore. They may perch on your shoulder and simply refuse to get off. They may also just lean in when you try to push them away from an object you do not want them to have. These habits can be changed but with a lot of perseverance.

In any case, you must be fully prepared to accept all the personality traits of the bird, whether they are good or bad. This is when you will be able to establish a realistic relationship with your bird. The more you learn the body language and the habits of the bird, the easier it will be for you to change these quirks for the better.

5.Caiques in aviculture
Caiques are gaining a lot of popularity in aviculture. The most popular birds are the black headed Caiques as these were the first species to be bred in captivity. However, the white bellied Caiques are catching up quite fast in terms of popularity.

When raised properly, they are known to form very close bonds with humans. As you have already read, these birds are also extremely friendly and playful. They love to play with toys and will also spend a lot of time displaying antics like laying on their back and playing with

13

toys. This behavior is very unusual for any species of birds. Caiques will simply roll over and will play lying on their back. This is called wrestling.

Caiques are not the best at flying and will often show a lot of fatigue after just flying for a short time period. They are slow and can be very clumsy in comparison to other parrot species. They would rather hop, jump, climb or simply walk to get from one place to another. Their strong legs and feet make them exceptional climbers. This is fun to watch when you give them toys like ladders.

Another peculiar behavior displayed by Caiques is called surfing. This is when they will rub their face, chest and wings on objects around them, mostly towels, carpets, paper, human hair, curtains or cushions. They will use the beak to pull themselves while doing so. While showing this behavior, they will often wrestle while laying on the back.

This behavior is believed to be a way of cleansing or bathing in Caiques. This is seen in both male and female birds. In the wild Caiques will show surfing behavior with wet leaves which, lead to the belief that it is a way of cleaning.

When raised in captivity, they will start to breed before they are three years of age. They will lay a small clutch that consists of a maximum of four eggs. The incubation period is about 27 days.

Caiques are not the best parents and the breeding pair will often find it hard to raise all the four chicks. The last chick that hatches will probably not survive unless you intervene to co-parent them or hand rear them.

Feeding is a responsibility that both parents will take up. The family remains in the nest box for about 75 days. Even though they seem to struggle, the parents are extremely affectionate towards their chicks. Once the chicks have fledged, they will still fly back to the nesting box and the whole family will roost there together. This is also quite uncommon for other species of parrots.

6.Consevation status
Not all the sub species are marked as endangered. The white bellied Caiques seem to be more in danger of extinction than the other

species. This has led to a ban on the export of these birds in most parts of South America. Today, there are only two small countries, namely Guyana and Surinam that continue to export these birds.

In order to preserve the numbers of these birds, several aviculturists are breeding other species of Caiques such as the yellow thighed Caiques. For the most part, it is the white bellied and the black headed Caiques that are bred. It has been noted that even the green thighed Caiques are breeding increasingly well in captivity. Although they are fewer in number in North America, it is likely that their popularity will increase with more success in breeding them.

In fact, zoos like the Sao Paulo Zoo in Brazil are breeding these sub species in large numbers. Green thighed Caiques are also being bred in South Africa and Europe.

Human activity remains the number one threat to the conservation of these birds. Fires in the forest are common due to human activity. The smoke caused by these fires are restricting the areas that the birds are willing to live in. In fact, this also threatens the habitats of these birds.

Caiques and humans also seem to compete for the same types of foods. Overharvesting of wild palm fruits is making it necessary for the birds to look for foods in other places. That is why they begin to raid rice crops early in the day. In case of heavy dew or rainfall, the birds get soaked and become unable to fly. That is when they are captured and consumed as a delicacy by the locals.

Poverty in these regions is also one factor that is threatening the existence of these birds. The locals not only rely on the birds as a source of food but will also hunt the birds down for the beautiful feathers. These feathers are exported for heavy prices. Ornaments are also made for sale using the plumes of these birds.

With an increase in the population of the indigenous people in these regions, Caiques are failing to survive in the wild. The good news, however, is that there is a good awareness about the need to conserve the environment of these birds. That is why the governments in South America, particularly Brazil have made more stringent laws with respect to birds. Today, it is illegal to sell or even keep these birds or any other native species.

With the efforts to keep these birds from becoming extinct, there seems to be more hope for them.

Chapter 2: Sourcing Caiques

Once you have decided to bring a Caique home, the next step is to understand where you can bring a bird home from. There are several options when it comes to sourcing your birds. We will discuss them all at length in this chapter.

1.Buying from a breeder

With Caiques becoming more popular in captivity, there has also been an increase in the number of individuals breeding these birds. One of the simplest ways to get a Caique is to contact a local breeder.

When you are buying from a breeder, remember that you must find one who really cares about the well-being of these birds and breeds them under humane conditions.

Finding a local breeder

It is easy to find a list of local breeders in your area. The hard part is making sure that they are 'good' breeders. You can begin by looking at classified ads for birds on sale. If you find any listing promising, you can contact the breeder.

Today, you have the option of looking online as well. There are various breeder directories that will list the best breeders in your city or even in your locality.

The other option is to contact bird clubs or local groups or even other Caique owners to find recommendations with respect to breeders. This is the best option, as you will get a firsthand account of their experience with the breeders that they suggest.

There are several exotic bird clubs that work towards protecting the interests of these birds. The individuals in these clubs are very passionate about the birds. In most cases, you will be able to find breeders within these clubs. They will not only help you find a healthy bird but will also be willing to help you raise the bird properly.

Interviewing the breeder

After you have located a good breeder in your area, you will have to make sure that you meet them or visit the facility. When you meet the breeder, you will be able to get a lot of information about the breeding practices and the general husbandry techniques of the breeder. That way, you will know if the birds are raised properly or not. Here are a few questions that you must ask during the breeder interview:

- How long have you been working with this particular species?
- Do you hand rear the birds?
- What do you feed the birds?
- How many times are the birds bred in a year?
- Who is your avian vet?

If the breeder is genuine and is concerned about the welfare of the birds, he will be able to answer these questions confidently. They will often be very enthusiastic about showing off their facility and will actually be proud of each bird that has been produced in the facility.

As you talk to the breeder, you will know by their eagerness to share their knowledge with you whether you want to associate with them or not. Any hesitation in answering queries should be a warning sign. Make sure that you do not encourage improper husbandry as the breeder is only looking to make quick bucks at the expense of the bird.

Examine the facility
Depending upon the breeder, you may or may not be allowed to check out the breeding area of the bird. In some cases, breeders follow a closed aviary practice where there are several guidelines to make sure that the flock is safe from any exposure to diseases. These are the best places to buy your bird from.

Note that a breeder who works in a closed aviary facility will also provide a health certificate for your bird. They will also be keen on helping you raise the birds in the right environment.

In case you have the opportunity to examine the facility, here are a few things that you must look out for:

- The cages should be clean. Cages that have feces on the floor, feathers on the bars and in the food bowls and a general appearance of being unkempt are a red flag. Good breeders will make sure that their birds are raised in a clean and healthy environment. This is done to reduce the risk of infections and diseases.

- The quality of food should be good. The birds must be given a variety of foods that are clean and fresh. If the breeder is only giving the birds seeds and pellets, it is not the best sign. You can take a look at the food bowl to get a hint. The birds must also get fresh produce as a part of their diet.

- The birds should be healthy. Usually Caiques are curious and will approach you when you go close to the cage. They should look alert and active. If you see that the birds look frightened and sickly and live in a dirty environment, leave immediately. It is never a good idea to buy a bird from negligent breeders as they come with several health issues.

Once you have found a breeder that you feel comfortable with, the next step is to negotiate all the terms of the sale. The breeder may have special conditions for the buyers or may still be hand feeding the birds. So, do not expect to take the bird home right away.

If you do have to wait to bring the bird home, make the most of this time to prepare your home for the new bird. That includes setting up the housing area, stocking up on the food, getting the bird some toys and even preparing your family for the new bird. The more you prepare, the less stressful the transition will be.

Make sure that you ask for a health certificate for your bird. It is also a good idea if the breeder wants to be able to be involved in the growth and development of the bird. This is a good sign that shows that the breeder genuinely cares. If you are a new bird owner, this can be very beneficial for you. You will get a lot of tips to make sure that the bird is healthy. You can also contact the breeder in case you have any queries with respect to your bird. They will become your source for all the information you need about the bird.

2.Adopting a Caique
The most cost effective way of getting a Caique is to adopt one. You have the option of choosing from several birds that have been abandoned or rescued from several situations.

Adoption may be difficult if it is your first time. There are several questions such as how the process works or how much it may cost. Also you can adopt from a rescue or from a shelter. These two options are vastly different from one another and in this chapter we will explore the process and all the options you have in more detail.

Adopting from shelter

A shelter is any public facility such as the city shelter or the county shelter. The pound, police and health departments and animal control are other examples of shelters. There are a few private facilities like the SPCA or other "humane societies" that you can find in your locality.

All these organizations are run independently or are government aided. These facilities have dedicated staff members and also have fixed working hours. In some of these organizations, you will have volunteers who will help you with the adoption process.

There are several online sites like adopt-a-pet.com that will list the birds and animals available for adoption in your locality. You will find the business hours of the shelters near you along with a proper listing of the adoption procedure. You can pay a visit during their business hours. Usually, your phone calls may go unanswered, as these shelters are really understaffed. If you see a Caique that you like, the best thing is to visit the shelter immediately.

Every adoption shelter has a different procedure. But for the most part, they all have some similar rules. These are the general rules that apply when you are planning to adopt a bird:

- First look for a bird that you want to adopt from the website of a shelter or from websites that provide listings.

- Make sure you visit the shelter to see the pet. You can enquire at the desk if you can have a few hours of interaction with the bird. This will help you understand the temperament and whether you are going to be able to handle the bird or not.

- The adoption fee is usually between $25 and $125. This depends on the shelter that you adopt from. In case the bird required any medical attention for injuries or any ailment, the adoption fee might be higher. This is to make sure that the medical expenses are covered.

- You will have to provide them with a valid ID. In some shelters, house check is mandatory to make sure that there is no illegal trading or export of the bird and also to make sure that the bird will be safe. Other paperwork includes all the vaccination records and health records of the bird.

- With the paperwork in place, you will be able to take your new bird home.

It is advisable that you spend some time interacting with the bird in case you are new to the world of Caiques and parrots.

Adopting from a rescue
A rescue is usually a bird that is being fostered at someone's home or in a private boarding facility. If the facility is run by volunteers, you can look out for their adoption events that take place over the weekends.

If you are looking for adoption listings and you find a pet at a "rescue", then you can give them a call or send them an email. In case of facilities like a boarding, you may be asked to fill out an application that will help them understand if you meet all the necessary criteria to take the bird home.

Even with rescues, the process of adoption will vary. The general rules that are followed are:

- You will send an email to the rescue after you find their listing online or perhaps in a newspaper. In most cases, you will receive a call the very next day asking you to provide more details about yourself. You may even make any enquiry about the bird that you have in mind. If you feel like you are going to be able to take care of the bird, you can visit the facility, the rescue's home or even the weekend adoption event.

- You will have to go through a home check. After they visit your home, you will be given a call about whether you are a suitable owner for the bird or not.

21

- Once you have been confirmed as the individual adopting the bird, you will have to provide an ID and collect all the health reports and vaccination details of the bird.

- If the rescue has an adoption contract, you will have to sign it and pay the adoption fee, which is usually between $100 and $300.

What is the difference?

When you adopt from a shelter, you will not only be able to see the bird that you chose on the website but also several other birds that you may like to take home. The screening process in a shelter is less stringent and in some cases, you may be able to take the bird home right away.

If the price is something that concerns you, then a shelter is a lot cheaper an option in comparison to a rescue. The vet care fees, however, could be higher with a shelter.

With a rescue, you have the advantage of getting more details about the bird as they have received one on one attention in most cases. The rescue will be more involved in the screening process. This also means that you are most likely to find a bird that suits you better. While the adoption costs are higher in case of a bird that you bring home from the rescue, you will not have to worry about paying anything additionally for the medical costs or vet costs.

This will allow you to choose where you wish to adopt your pet from. Remember that birds in shelters may have a history of abuse or serious injury. That means that they may even have behavioral issues. If you are adopting from a shelter, it is better that you have some experience with either Caiques or at least with other parrots.

Why adoption?

With the growing popularity of the Caique parrot among pet owners, the breeding of this bird has also become very common. Not all Caique parrot breeders will provide the birds with environments that will help them thrive. In most cases, the birds are lonely and suffer a lot of hardship, as the breeders are not exactly sensitive towards the needs of the birds.

In order to make their own profits higher, the birds are weaned much earlier than the appropriate age. This is not a good idea, as the birds do not learn how to feed on their own. That becomes a hassle for new owners.

There are several Parrot Rescue Organizations that are dedicated to finding the right home for these birds. They will also help you find a bird that will be able to fit into your lifestyle. The reason most pet owners are skeptical about adoption is because they believe that birds in shelters or recue homes are unhealthy. This is far from the truth. In fact, in many cases, the birds are given up because the owners are unable to afford appropriate care for the bird, because they had to move or because there has been a death in the family. In some cases, enthusiastic buyers without much knowledge on the bird will simply give up as they are not able to cope with the responsibility.

It is definitely a far more noble option to adopt a bird. If you can give them a loving home, then it is the right way to go.

3.Buying from a pet store

Often the easiest way to get a bird that you want is to buy one from a pet store. While pet stores are not all bad and there are still several pet stores that work towards keeping the environment for the birds healthy and happy. This should be your last option.

There are some issues that are very common with pet stores. Here are the top reasons why pet stores are not the best bet in most cases:

- While not all pet stores bring in their parrots or other pets from pet factories, they are associated with them. You need to find out why the breeder did not sell the bird himself. You may find that the pet store owner breeds parrots or that they have a tie up with a breeder who does not have the time to make the sale.

  However, in most cases, breeders give up on the weaker birds and sell them off to pet stores. So, the low quality birds make their way in to the pet store.

- Pet store bought birds may have several individual problems. This can stem from the fact that they have not been hand tamed, they do not have the right environment to develop in or because they do not receive as much mental stimulation as required.

23

- These birds are not handled well when they are transferred from the aviary to the pet shop or from the pet shop to a new home. This causes a lot of issues.

- Pet stores are very noisy. There are other animals and birds out there. In addition to that, they may not have enough light, the right diet or may be disturbed by too much handling by potential buyers.

- Birds are abruptly removed from their cage, separated from cage mates and then sent off to new homes. This is very stressful for these birds.

While these issues may not seem too serious to most of us, the fact is that parrots are very intelligent and highly cognitive. It is particularly important to make sure that these birds get the right care.

However, if you must buy from a pet store, here are some things that you should keep in mind:
- The cages should be clean.
- The food and water bowls should be hygienic.
- The birds must be active and responsive when you approach them.
- The pet store staff should have ample information about the species that they are trying to sell to you. You can confirm this by asking questions about the diet, the habitat and the behavior of Caiques. Do your homework so that you know if they are giving you the right information.

When you have all these criteria in place, make sure that you carefully transfer the bird to your home to reduce stress. We will discuss about that in detail in the next chapter so you can make the bird's ride home a pleasant one.

4.Are you ready for the bird?
It is a common misconception that birds are not as much maintenance and work as other pets such as dogs. When you are bringing a Caique home, remember that these birds are extremely sensitive and need a good ambience to develop properly.

If you have decided to buy or adopt a bird, you need to make sure that you are ready. Only when you know for sure should you venture into this responsibility. Here are a few questions you should ask yourself before you bring a Caique home:

- Are you willing to make a lifelong commitment to the bird? Remember that they will live up to about 40 years. How do you see your life after these years?

- Will you be able to set aside time to prepare your bird's food everyday? This includes providing fresh vegetables and other healthy food options to your bird. Only a seed or pellet diet is not sufficient.

- Do you have the time to play and interact with your bird? How much time are you willing to give the bird each day where you take him or her out of the cage and engage in activities together?

- Can you afford to get the bird regular vet exams? You must be able to take the bird for an annual check-up even if he seems to be in perfect health.

- Do you have enough space in your home? A Caique is a medium sized bird but they need a good housing area where they can flap their wings, play and rest. A small cage in a corner is definitely not an option.

- If you do get bitten by the bird, what will you do? If you are afraid of this, you must reconsider bringing a bird home. There may be some accidents, particularly with Caiques. If that puts the bird at the risk of being abandoned, then you must reconsider bringing one home in the first place.

- Are you ready to clean the cage regularly? Never let the poop and other dirt build up on the floor, as the bird will always be at the risk of falling ill.

- Are you okay with getting some bird poop on the floor, couch, table or maybe your favorite shirt? It is possible to potty train the bird but until then, these accidents may happen.

- Is it okay for the bird to be noisy at times? Parrots of all kinds may get noisy at dawn and dusk. This is their instinct. If you have neighbors who may complain, make sure that you have their consent. In addition to that, you and your family should be up for some noise and screeching from time to time.

- Are you willing to make lifestyle changes? There are several things like air fresheners, Teflon pans, ceiling fans and scented candles in our homes that may be hazardous to the bird? Are you willing to make modifications and changes to make your house a safe haven for the bird?

Only when you have satisfactory answers to these questions should you bring a bird home. A beautiful and intelligent bird like a Caique must never be turned into a trophy. They need your time and attention just as much as every other pet does. So, once you make a commitment, you should be able to stick to it.

5.Choosing a healthy bird

When you bring a bird home, make sure that he is healthy. You can even ask for a vet examination and a health certificate from a breeder or pet store before you take the bird home.

Even if the bird is carrying a pathogen, it can be risky. If you have other birds at home, you are putting them at risk as well. When you are unable to tell if the bird is healthy, you might be getting yourself into some trouble. Caring for a sick bird will demand a lot of time and can even be expensive. In any case, no one wants to lose a pet to health issues.

Here are some tips that will help you identify a healthy bird:

- The eyes must be clear. If they are cloudy, red or unusual in appearance, it is a sign of some health issue.

- Development of the feet and the beak is the first sign of the bird's health. If you see protrusions, bumps, discoloration or other abnormalities in the feet and beak it is a good idea to look for another bird.

- The feathers must be intact. Unless the bird is molting, bald spots on the body is an unhealthy sign. The feathers must also not appear pale and discolored. If you see that the bird's feathers look untidy and ruffled, then there are chances that he has not been taken proper care of. The wings must never droop as they indicate lethargy and possible illnesses.

- The bird should be active. Caiques in particular love to climb, swing on perches and even fly around in the cage. If the bird is huddled up in a corner or if he remains close to the floor of the cage at all times, it means that he has some health issues.

- The bird must be responsive when you approach. Caiques are curious by nature and will approach you when you get close to the cage. If the bird seems to retreat or if he becomes very nippy or aggressive, you can take them as signs of behavioral issues. It also may mean that the bird has not been hand tamed.
Make sure that you bring the bird home after checking his health completely. If you can get a health guarantee, then you can be sure that you are bringing a good specimen into your home.

When you have found a bird with these qualities, you may bring him home.

Chapter 3: Bringing the Caique Home

When you have chosen the bird that you want for your home, the next step is to make sure that you help the bird make the transition into the new home comfortably. This means that you need to be prepared entirely to make your home the perfect space for the bird.

Taking safety measures, making sure that you have all the supplies in place and also keeping your family informed about the requirements of the bird are part of the responsibilities of a Caique owner.

1.Bird proofing your home

The first thing that you need to do is ensure that your home is safe to keep the Caique in. There are several things in our home that we may take for granted but can actually be very dangerous for the bird that you plan to bring into your home. Here are some safety measures that you need to take:

- Make sure that you give the bird good quality air to breathe. Any preservative sprays, aerosols, kerosene or gas heaters, cigarettes etc. should be kept away from the bird's cage. If the air is not of good quality, it causes a lot of stress to the bird and may lead to issues like feather plucking.

- All electrical cords must be hidden or put inside insulated beading. That way there is no chance that the bird may chew on the cord and get electrocuted.

- If you have a humidifier at home, it should be kept in check. While the bird itself will benefit from an increased level of humidity, these gadgets are often home to bacteria if not maintained properly. It is a good idea to install humidifiers that have UV lights to kill any fungi and bacteria.

- If you are using any "fog" producing insecticides to take care of fleas and other insects, make sure that you have removed the cacique from the cage before you do so. The house must be aired fully before you bring the bird in. In any case, consult your avian vet before bringing a pesticide home.

- The kitchen is one of the most dangerous areas in your house. The bird must be kept out of the kitchen at all times. Installing a door may be a good idea. There are hot stoves, pots, cooking fumes and ovens that can be very hazardous to your bird. Teflon cookware releases fumes that can be fatal to birds. Make sure that you get rid of Teflon if you are unable to keep the bird far away from the kitchen.

- Keep your bird away from any items that may contain lead. This includes jewelry, fishing weights, wires, paint, stained glass, zippers, light bulbs, foil from champagne bottles, antiques and several other things. Lead poisoning leads to toxicosis in birds can sometimes lead to issues like feather plucking in the initial stages.

- Some medicines prescribed for humans can be fatal for birds. You must keep all your medication in cabinets or in boxes that cannot be accessed by your Caique.

- Keep doors and windows closed when the bird is out of the cage. Even the lapse of a second may lead to your bird escaping. It can be really frightening to you and the bird. If your birds have just learnt to fly, make sure that there is some marking, such as a wind chime, before closed windows and mirrors to prevent your bird from crashing into them.

- When you are placing any plant near the cage of the bird, be wary of the chance of it being poisonous to your bird. You can ask your vet to give you a list of all the household plants that are safe to have in your home with your Caique being around.

- Scented products like deodorants, fabric softeners and others can cause respiratory issues in birds. When you clean your bird's cage and the area around it, avoid using these products.

- Water is one of the biggest hazards for your bird. Drowning is an accident that can occur in seconds. When you are cleaning the house with a bucket of water, fill your tub or even leave the toilet, make sure that the bird is away from water sources. The lid on your toilet seat should always be closed and so should pots and buckets.

- Never give your bird household items to play with. Keep keys, pens, pencils, children's toys and other items away from your bird. These items may contain toxic products that will cause severe problems for your bird.

- Keep the temperature in your house in control. Sudden changes in temperature can lead to issues. Icy blasts from your air conditioner or the heat from radiators can be harmful to the bird. While they can cope with gradual changes in temperature, sudden changes can lead to over heating or even freezing. The bird will show signs like panting, holding the wings close or away from the body and excessive water consumption to indicate temperature changes that are not comfortable.

- Ceiling fans and table fans are risky to have on when the bird is out of the cage. You must never let the bird get too close as the wings may get clipped or caught in the fan. In some cases, these accidents can be fatal.

- Another metal that is very harmful for birds is zinc. Quick links or metal fittings on toys, the powder coat on cages and other metal objects like taps can be the most common source of zinc. Zinc toxicity causes health issues like feather plucking in birds.

Caiques have this uncanny ability to get into trouble. Their curiosity coupled with their high levels of energy is usually the perfect recipe for disaster. So, make sure that you are vigilant and that you keep an eye on your bird.

These are the basic bird proofing methods. If there are some specific areas in your home that have caused any trouble to your bird, you need to take adequate measures to keep your bird away.

2.Setting up the cage
Make sure that the housing area of the bird is fully set up before you bring him home. That will make the transition much easier. You can

keep the bird in the permanent housing area from day 1 instead of adding to the stress of moving to a new cage just after the bird has gotten used to the new home.

Size and interiors of the cage
Caiques are birds that love to play and move around. So it is necessary that you provide them with a large enough cage that allows them to do so.

For a Caique, the minimum size of the cage should be 24x24x20inches. The cage should be wide enough to make sure that you can include as many accessories and toys as possible. The way to check if the size is good enough for your bird is that he should be able to stretch his wings in all directions without touching the bars of the cage.

In case you decide to keep a pair of birds, then you definitely need a larger cage. You also need to make sure that you have a spare cage in order to keep the birds separately in case one of them falls sick or if the birds show any aggression towards one another during the breeding season.

The cage can be lined with newspaper, as it is the safest option for a substrate. If you plan to use wood shavings, then avoid redwood, pine and cedar as they give out certain hydrocarbons that are toxic. This can damage the respiratory tract of the bird. Aspen shaving is a good idea.

At the bottom of the cage, you can place a grate so that the droppings do not collect on the floor. However, sometimes there are deposits on the grate that you will have to remove periodically. Otherwise, it will become uncomfortable for the bird to walk on the floor.

Never use any pine shavings, corn cobs, walnut shells or cedar shavings on the floor as substrate. They can cause irritation to the bird and can even lead to some allergic symptoms. The best option is clean and dry grass, aspen shavings or non-toxic sawdust. If you are using wood chips, choose the larger ones so that the birds do not ingest them accidentally.

Newspaper, brown paper bags or paper towels are the best option to cover the floor. These materials are easy to change, provide best absorption and are also the most economical way to go when you have to monitor droppings of your bird on a regular basis.

Avoid placing any food dish holders in your bird's cage as the birds can get stuck in the openings of these holders. Even when you are snapping the feeder cups in, you should be careful as the wings can get stuck when you snap it in place. Even the toes and legs can get stuck when they are trying to eat. The best option is to place ceramic or plastic bowls of good quality on the floor of the cage. Birds may perch on the metal holders and can get seriously injured if the design is not up to the mark.

Using a water bottle or any other watering device is not necessary unless your bird has the habit of pooping in the water or dirtying the water with their feathers. The traditional watering dishes are the best option as they are also easy to clean. This also ensures that the birds get to drink enough water. Dehydration must be prevented at all costs as it is the leading cause for deaths in captive birds.

You must make sure that the cage has several perches for the bird to rest on or for the bird to play on. Some of the most common materials for the perch include:

- Ropes: these are the easiest ones to install and can be fun for the bird.

- Wood: Apple wood, maple and madrone wood perches are the safest option for parrots.

- PVC- only choose plumber grade PVC as it is safe for the birds.

- Acrylic- only get an acrylic perch if it has been sanded on the surface. If the perch is too slippery, it will lead to issues with the bird's toes.
- Sand or concrete perches- these perches may be the best option as they keep the nails of the bird trim and also let the bird sharpen the beak.

Cage safety
It is not enough that your cage is large and well equipped with accessories. It is necessary to make sure that your bird is safe in the

cage. Here are some safety measure that you can take to keep your bird safe in the cage:

- Choose a rectangular cage as opposed to a round one. In case of the round cages, the birds do not have anywhere to hide or retreat into when they are scared. These cages will also affect the feathers of the bird, especially the ones on the tail.

- It is best that you choose a powder coated or stainless steel cage. Others that are made of wrought iron or with a painted surface can be dangerous as they may have deposits of zinc or lead.

- The bars should be parallel all over the cage. They must not converge anywhere.

- The distance between two bars must be appropriate. The width must be such that the bird is not able to fit his head through them and should not be so small that the toes get stuck.

- Make sure that the bars are made of a strong enough material to withstand the bite from your Caique, who will use his beak to climb up and down.

- If you are using any towels or covering material on the cage, then you should make sure that there are no threads or holes in them. This may lead to strangulation or may have the bird's toenails or legs entangled leading to fractures or injuries.

- The cage should not have any protrusions or sharp edges. If your bird scrapes his body on these protrusions, it can lead to severe injuries that may cause infections.

Toys form an important part of the cage set up of your bird. There are several types of toys that you can choose from for your Caique. In the next section we will discuss all the options and their benefits in detail.

Toys for the cage
If there is one thing that Caique parrots love to do, it is to play all day. They need adequate mental stimulation in order to be healthy and happy. This can only be achieved when you have enough toys for the

birds. There are a variety of toys that you can include to keep the bird engaged all day long.

Caiques love to explore with their beaks. For this reason, they need to have toys that will last longer. The toys should also be sturdier in comparison to a toy that you may buy for a smaller bird. It is best that you choose toys made from plastic or any acrylic material. You will be able to find exclusive shredding and chewing toys that are actually good for the birds.

Toys made from safe woods like aspen and birch will satisfy the chewing needs of the birds. There are also toys that are made from rope or any other digestive material that is safe even if your bird accidentally swallows a few bits. Leather is also a great option when it comes to chewing toys. You can either mount or hand these toys as long as you keep all the safety aspects in mind.

One feature that is unique to Caique parrots is that they love to lie down on their backs when they play. They are the only type of parrot for whom you can buy foot toys. These are small toys that they can hold in their feet and play with. You can find them with most toy stores or can make them with older toys after removing any hazardous parts. Some of the most popular foot toys include small balls, pieces of wood, teething toys used for babies and other soft material.

What you need to ensure with toys that you buy for your Caiques is variety. There should be a variety of textures, colors, shapes and sizes. These birds are extremely mentally active and will get easily bored with monotony. So, you must try to rotate the toys every week in order to keep them interested.

You can even move the toys around to provide some variety to the birds. You will know that your bird is bored of a certain toy when you see it lying in one end of the room without the bird even noticing it.

Observing your bird's playtime can give you a lot of clues about what he likes or dislikes. If he is fond of a certain type of toy and is inclined to playing with that more often, then you can bring in more varieties of that toy, maybe different textures and sizes.

For example, if your bird likes the swings then you can choose from a variety of swings made from wood, beads or rope. Having more than one type of the toy gives you the advantage of moving it around to keep your bird interested in it for a longer time.

Because your Caique is going to spend a lot of time with his toys, it is mandatory to take all the necessary precautions to keep him safe. The danger of getting entangled and suffocating is real with a Caique.

The issue of entangling is common with toys that are suspended. If the toy is suspended using a chain link, then you need to make sure that the link is large enough for the whole body of the bird to pass through or it should be so small that the bird cannot even get his toe through it.

The length of the suspended toy also matters a lot. You need to make sure that the length is not more than that which can wrap around your thumb once. If the length is too long, the bird can hang from it when entangled. If you notice that the exposed length is more than this, you can take precautions by either tying knots or by tying other small trinkets along the length of the twine or rope.

You need to make sure that any toy or perch that has ropes or twines attached to it does not have any fray that can wrap around the toe of the bird. In many cases, the toes of the bird will get entangled and can actually break or tear.

The attachment that you use for the toy is also very important. The most dangerous one for the beak of the bird is the split ring or the key ring. These rings are easily opened by the bird using the beak. Then, you have the risk of the ring going through the beak or the risk of the beak getting stuck in it. Even with carabineers the beak of the bird can get mutilated.

The best option to suspend the bird's toys is a C-clasp. The screw type closing mechanism will reduce any chance of the beak getting trapped in it. Pinching of the beak or the toe is also less likely to occur with these clasps.

It is true that the rope type or suspended type of toys pose the biggest risk for a Caique. However, you must never neglect the small foot toys. These toys may have small parts that are likely to break and cause choking in case the bird swallows it accidentally.

Non-natural parts of any toy that you think can be chewed up or bitten will pose the serious threat of intestinal blockage in case it is swallowed accidentally.

You can get really creative with the toys. Making foraging toys using paper and treats is a great idea. You can even recycle an old toy as long as you keep the safety measures in mind. Now, if your bird has destroyed a toy completely, it is a sign that he has thoroughly enjoyed it.

Placement of the cage

Where you put the cage will also matter in keeping the bird comfortable in the cage. Here are a few pointers that will help you with this:

- The cage should be kept in a quiet spot in the house, free from any distraction. A corner wall is the perfect place with the cage resting against the wall. This will make the bird feel very secure.

- The bird must be able to see the activities in your household from his cage. If he is secluded, then he can be easily startled. Caiques learn everything about their new home through observation. So, you can keep him in a corner that allows him to see you and your family for the most part. But, he must not be right in the middle of all the action, as it will become a little stressful for him.

- The cage should be away from noise. So, a room that is facing a road with too much traffic is not the best idea. He will always be alert and can even get frightened with the noise during the day or the lights of the vehicles zipping around at night.

- The area around the cage also matters. Make sure that there is no cemented surface or concrete surface near the cage. This will increase the chance of serious injuries should your bird accidentally fall out of the cage or fall when he is let out of the cage.

- The cage must be away from the air conditioner, heater and the kitchen. Sudden fluctuations of temperature and the fumes from these areas can lead to health issues such as respiratory problems.

It will also stress the bird out which will lead to behavioral issues like plucking of his feathers.

- Ample light is necessary for birds from the tropical areas. If you live in an area that does not allow the bird to get a lot of natural light, you must provide the bird with a full spectrum of artificial light. This is crucial in the development of the bird as it keeps his body clock aligned.

The placement of the cage is crucial in helping your bird make an easy transition into your home. The more opportunity he has to retreat and rest, the easier it will become for him to adjust to his new home and all the members of his new flock.

3.Making the transition

Once your home is bird proofed and the housing area is in place, the next step is to make sure that your bird is able to have a stress free transition into its new home. There are a few measures that you can take to make this happen.

The most important part of making the transition is to get the ride from the breeder, the rescue or the shelter to your home right. The smell and the sounds of a car can be rather stressful for a bird. Here are some tips that can make the bird's ride home easier:

- Take a transfer cage with the appropriate bedding material with you. You may need more bedding if the ride is longer.

- The bird must be given enough water and food through the trip. It is advisable that you stop every 20 minutes in case of a long ride back home to check if the bird needs any water or food.

- The temperature within the car should be maintained at room temperature. You must not keep any windows open, as the drafts can be really stressful for the bird.

- Covering the cage with a cloth is a good idea. Place a cloth or blanket over half the surface of the cage. That way if the bird wants to hide or rest, he will have a cozy place to do so.

- Do not play any music in the car. You must also not have loud conversations when you are transferring the bird. It is best that you do not talk to the bird as he already has too many new sounds around him. If you must address your bird, do so in a soft and soothing voice.

Once the bird has arrived in your home, the next step is to get him accustomed to the new home. Here are the steps that you must follow when the bird has arrived:

- Place the bird's transfer cage in front of his permanent cage with the doors facing each other. Keep the doors open and let the bird hop in on his own. If he does not enter the cage for more than ten minutes, lure him in with a treat.

- Once the bird is in his new home, shut the door and leave him to himself. You can place a blanket over half the cage surface. Then, you can leave the bird alone and allow him to figure things out for himself.

- The only interaction that you will have with the bird is when you feed him or when you change the water. Do not talk to the bird on the first day and refrain from introducing too many people to him. When you are around the cage, make sure that you are crouched to stay at the eye level of the bird. Towering over the cage will make him wary of you, as he will think of you as a predator.

Caiques are very cautious by nature. This is probably because they are prey animals and have the natural instinct to be aware all the time. In addition to this, they are highly cognitive beings. That is why you must not interact with the bird too much till you notice him being more comfortable in his new environment.

What not to do
It does not matter whether you are a first time bird owner or if you have had birds in your home in the past. It is always the nature of human beings to make the bird feel "at home" or "as part of the family" from day one.

This, unintentionally, puts a lot of stress and pressure on the new bird. It is very easy for us to overlook the fears that the bird experiences when he is in a new home amidst all the excitement of actually bringing home a beautiful bird such as the Caique.

Here are some of the most common mistakes that we make:

- We tend to play with the bird for long hours. Cuddling, comforting, kissing or touching are human ways of telling the bird that you love him. But, this is a whole new experience for your feathered friend and is probably scaring him.

- We forget that everything in our home is unfamiliar to the bird. If you really look at it from the bird's point of view, it might make sense. One minute they are with a breeder, then they are put in a cage and have to endure the unfamiliar sensations in the car. When they are released into the new home, they actually have no idea where they are. Animals and birds are most sensitive to smell and sound. The bird is not able to get one familiar sight, sound or smell from the time he enters your home. You probably have a cat or dog. While the pet is away from the cage, the lingering smell is something that the bird will catch immediately. Imagine the horror of living so close to a predator, especially when you are a member of the lower rung of the food chain.

- We love to show our new pets off. This means that you probably have a lot of people over. The bird is put in the midst of so many strange faces and smells. If the bird is handled by strangers, you are simply making the transition worse for your beloved pet.

- We keep the house noisy with the music systems and the TV. For the first few days, it is a good idea to keep the volume low on all your appliances till the bird is able to ignore the sounds produced and is able to play comfortably.

- If the bird has been hand tamed, chances are that he will hop on to your finger when you present it. This should never be considered an invitation for petting. As a rule, a bird is uncomfortable with the idea of being handled by a stranger. When the bird is ready for physical interaction he will let you know by rubbing against your hand or by lowering his head before you. We will learn in detail about the body language of the bird. For the first few days, let the bird perch on your finger without you making any attempt to touch or pet him.

When you have a bird in your home, apply the no hands rule for a few days. You can spend some time with your bird with your hands on the sides of the cage. Then the bird will approach your hands and try to get more familiar.

The less we force the bird to become our companions, the easier it will be for them to actually play that role. When you leave them alone, allow them to explore and then respond. You will be making the transition completely stress free for your beloved new bird.

4.Introducing the bird to your family

Your family may consist of other pets as well. While there are strict rules for the human members of your family to meet the new bird, there are also many pointers that you need to keep in mind when you are introducing your bird to your cats, dogs or perhaps other feathered friends.

Rules for your family

Caiques will usually form a bond with the whole family but will have one family member who they share the strongest bond with. Now, there are a few rules that you will have to follow when you introduce your family to a new bird:

- The person who has brought the bird home will be the one doing most of the handling till the bird is used to the family. This includes feeding and watering the bird for the first few days.

- Children must be strictly told not to tease the bird or try to play with it. Caiques are birds that will bite when threatened. This is purely for the safety of your child.

- Do not leave brightly colored objects near the bird's housing area. This includes toys, clothes or any large item that can scare the poor bird.

- Verbal communication should be kept to a minimum with the new bird. The family must strive to keep the environment of the bird as calm and comforting as possible. This means that they will not show off the bird to friends until the bird is ready.

- No pictures with the bird. When you are trying to get a selfie with your new bird or are trying to take a picture of the bird, he becomes very aware of the fact that something is going on. Added to that, you may turn the flash on or the jazzy cover of your phone may scare the bird.

- The family will ease their way into the bird's heart. This will include just standing near the cage with the hands on the sides for a few minutes. Make sure the person is at eye level to prevent the bird from feeling like he is being attacked by a predator.

- No loud noises in the room that you have stationed your bird in.

With these rules, you will prevent any accidents with respect to the bird. Children, especially, should be taught to treat the bird with a lot of respect. Caiques are curious and may approach the child sometimes. If he or she screams or scares the bird, there is a chance of a serious bite. It is best that you never leave the child unsupervised around a new bird.

Introduction to pets
If you have a cat or dog at home, ask yourself if you really want to introduce them without any barriers. It doesn't matter how gentle your cat or dog is, the sheer size difference is cause for concern when you are introducing a bird to your cat or dog.

You must also never forget that your cat or dog is a natural predator for a bird. This will make it extremely stressful for your Caique and may lead to stress related issues like feather plucking if the interactions are not monitored.

The first thing you need to make sure is that the cage is in a part of the house that does not allow the cat or dog to climb over it. Even if the pet cannot reach in, this act itself can be traumatizing for the bird. It can also lead to accidents like the cage falling over, which will also put your pet at the risk of injuries.

If you must introduce them, you can do so after the bird has settled in in the new house. When they are able to interact with you without any signs of stress, it is time to introduce them to their furry pals.

Place the cage in a room that the pet spends most of his or her time in. Watch your bird's reaction and the reaction of the pet. If the response is violent in the form of loud barking or growling, put the bird back and let him relax. Do this a couple of times till the bird is not interesting to your pet anymore.

You will know this when you place the cage in the room and your cat or dog simply won't respond to the bird. Now taking the bird out of the cage at this point is still not advisable unless you are fully ready.

For the bird to be let out of the cage, you must be able to handle him and pick him up in a jiffy in case there is a negative response from the pet towards the bird. If the bird has not been hand tamed yet, you can certainly not let him meet the pet outside the cage.

You can try to get the bird and the pet to interact in any open area when you are supervising. If they are calm, then you can let them explore the new scents and sounds. But, while cat and dog bites are severely damaging to the bird, it has been reported that a threatened Caique has injured dogs and cats with a sharp bite or peck.

This is why you must always make sure that the bird is secure in the cage when you have to leave the house. Even if the interactions in your presence have been calm and relaxed, it does not mean that your pet and the Caique can be great buddies. If the instincts do kick in, you may come home to the most terrifying scene and you have no one to blame but yourself.

Introduction to other birds
If you have other birds in your home, the first step is quarantining the new bird. This means that the bird will be placed in a separate cage, away from the other birds for at least 30 days. This is the time period that any disease that the bird might be carrying needs to manifest. You must also be sure that you never handle your existing flock after handling the new bird without washing and disinfecting your hands.

Introductions can begin by placing the new bird in a separate cage next to the cage of your existing bird or birds. If the birds respond with loud screeching and a lot of noise, let them be. They will settle down in a while.

Let them stay in the same room for a few days to get used to each other's presence. Then, you can try to make the introductions to your flock.

In your flock, there is an obvious pecking order. You will notice that one bird is the most dominant one of all and another one is most submissive. Allow the submissive bird to meet the new bird first. It is best that you let the birds out so that they are in neutral territory. If you put the submissive bird in the cage of the new one, he may get territorial and aggressive.

When these birds are comfortable in each other's presence, it is time to introduce the next bird in the order of dominance leading up to the most dominant one. In neutral areas, fights are less likely to happen. If they do occur, it is best that you put the birds back in separate cages.

When you have a mixed aviary, it is a good idea to keep birds that are similar in size together. The small bird can get really intimidated by a bird that is too large. You must also avoid housing birds that are closely related to prevent any chances of hybridization.

There must be additional feeding stations as well as water sources. In case one of the birds is very dominant and aggressive, he may control all the sources of food and water if there is just one available.

Separate the area within the cage using sleeping tents or plant covers. This will give the meek bird a place to hide in. Then, when you spot the problem, you will be able to help the bird in case he is unable to protect himself.

You may want to keep pairs of the same species to promote breeding. Avoid having more than one pair unless you plan to have a flock of the same birds.

The birds must be checked upon everyday to see if there are any signs of fighting or chasing. The birds that are being attacked should be placed in a separate cage immediately.

5.Proper quarantining techniques

Quarantining is one of the biggest responsibilities of pet owners. This is the first step towards defending your old flock and your new bird from the possibility of any health issues.

When you have a flock that has been living together for a while, they would have developed a unique environment that keeps them immune to certain germs that they may be exposed to on a regular basis. Now, it does not matter how impeccable the living conditions of your new bird were when you bought him, it is necessary to quarantine the bird.

Why is quarantining so important? Remember that you have displaced the bird from its old eco system and have brought him to a new environment that may contain several germs that he has not been exposed to. This is another causal factor for the stress that birds experience when they are moved to a new location.

The stress can either be very minor or can be major based on the nature of the bird you bring home. When the bird is stressed, the immune system becomes weak. This means that the bird may not be as healthy as he was when you bought him.

If you fail to quarantine the bird, you are exposing him to a plethora of new germs that he may fall victim to. If the bird becomes ill, he will shed the pathogenic germ in large amounts. In addition to that, he will also shed any germ that he may have brought in from his previous home. That means that the environment in your home has several pathogens that your birds are probably not immune to.

Even if there are no new germs, the volume of the old ones can be so high that the birds are unable to handle it. While the new and the old bird may fall sick, it is obvious that we believe that the new bird is responsible for the illness.

The truth is that an improper quarantining procedure is the cause for this poor immune response. You are able to control the stress that the bird is going through and his ability to cope with the new home when you quarantine your birds correctly. With a gradual and small amount of exposure to the shared ecosystem of the birds, the new one and the existing flocks will be able to build the immunity that they need.

Here are the correct steps to quarantine your birds so that they do not develop unwanted health issues. It does not matter if you are adopting the bird or fostering him temporarily, make sure that you do not neglect any steps:

- While a minimum of 30 days is recommended for quarantining, 6 weeks is the safe period to give the bird ample time to get used to the new environment.

- In this period, observe the bird carefully. There must not be any signs of illness such as lethargy, discharge from thee eyes or beak, unusually colored droppings, watery droppings etc.

- Watch the eating habits of the bird. When they are in a new environment, birds do find it traumatic and will stop eating. Then, you may offer him some treats that he likes. Drinking water, eating and having a normal poop is mandatory for the bird.

- Bring home a gram scale that will allow you to weigh the bird on a regular basis. Sudden weight loss is a cause for concern.

- If your bird is unwell, take him to the vet immediately. You will have to quarantine him until he tests negative for the most common parrot diseases. This might be longer than six weeks.

- Even when the bird is stable and healthy, arrange for a vet visit halfway through the quarantine period.

- The room that you choose for your bird should be away from the rest of the flock. Only birds that are brought in on the same day, from the same place can be placed in the same quarantining room.

- The quarantine room should have enough fresh air and good natural light. Avoid rooms that have a furnace or an air conditioner. These are sources of stress for the bird.

- The most important thing to keep in mind is that birds tend to hide their illness. So do not place the bird with the rest of the flock unless he is checked by a vet, even if he seems perfectly healthy.

- It is a good idea to have an apron in the quarantine room that you will use when you are handling the new bird. Make sure that you remove this apron and wash your hands thoroughly before you handle your existing flock.

- When the quarantined bird is being given any medication, the syringe or the feeder that you use should be kept away from the housing area of the existing flock.

- Once the new bird has settled in and the quarantine period has come to an end, discard any object such as a perch or a toy that you cannot sterilize.

- The food and water bowls of the quarantined bird should never be washed along with those belonging to the existing flock.

When you are done with the internal quarantining, make it a habit to quarantine your birds from any external source of infection. If you visit the zoo, visit other birds or reptiles, it is recommended that you take off the shoes that you have worn outside your home. The clothes that you have worn when you are visiting other birds should be washed and cleaned. Make sure that you wash your hands the moment you get home. This is true even if you are walking through a park that may have ducks or geese.

Our clothes and shoes can carry dander and droppings that will in turn carry several disease causing organisms.

The more precautions you take, the safer your birds will be.

Chapter 4: Caring for your Caique

Once the bird is in your home, you need to make sure that he has everything that he needs to be healthy and safe. Caring for a Caique involves more than just feeding the bird. You need to make sure that he has a life that is free from stress in any form.

1.Feeding

For the most part, the diet of Caiques in the wild includes fruits, nuts and seeds. The closer the diet of the bird is to what they consume naturally, the easier it is for them to absorb all the nutrients that are present in them. It is also easier for the bird to digest these foods.

Nutritional deficiencies can lead to a lot of health disorders, which we will discuss in the following chapters. To ensure that this is prevented, you have to make sure that you provide them with a variety of foods in their diet.

It is a good idea to feed your birds twice each day in small portions. Preparation of the food is key to making it easy on their digestive system. You also need to make sure that the food is always fresh and free from any form of contamination or spoilage.

Here are the foods that you can give your bird:

Fresh fruits and vegetables

Vegetable mix must be fresh at all times. You may store it for a maximum of three days when frozen. Some vegetables that you can add include peas, corn, shredded carrot, broccoli, zucchini, beets, yellow squash, cooked sweet potato, beets and greens like kale and spinach. Even adding a bit of lentils can work very well for the diet of your bird. If you have easy access to corn on the cob, cut it into wheels and provide it to your birds. It makes a great foraging idea.

You must add fresh fruit cut into small cubes. The fruits that you can give your bird include apples, grapes, pears, cantaloupe, oranges, mangos, bananas, berries, plums, papaya, mango, cherries, kiwi and star fruit.

When you are providing fruits with pits, make sure that the pit is removed fully. The pit can be poisonous to your bird. It is a good idea to have a small kitchen garden in your home if you have the space for it. That way you can provide your bird with fresh produce without the risk of any pesticides.

It is a good idea to soak the fruits and vegetables in some warm water before you give it to your bird. That way, it will have softened and will become much easier for your bird to digest it. Try as much variety as you can and eventually the birds will select their favorites.

Lentils and sprouted beans

You can give your bird dried lentils and sprouted beans. Soak the beans overnight so that they are sprouted. When you are sprouting the beans, makes sure that you wash the beans well and drain them a few times. Be careful not to damage any bean as it can get spoiled. You can mix a small amount of these beans with the vegetable mix and give it to your bird. When stored under the right conditions, these beans can be used for three days.

The bean options that you have include garbanzo beans, Canadian beans, mung beans and Chinese red peas.

Dry foods and seed

Several commercially prepared dried pellets and seeds are available for birds. You can provide your bird with the following options:

- Safflower based dried seeds
- Pumpkin seeds
- White striped sunflower

It is best that you avoid sunflower seeds as they are high in fats and are generally very poor in the nutrition content. You have several other dried food options besides the commercially available ones. Some of them are:

- Spray millet
- Cashew
- Walnuts
- Pistachio
- Almonds

48

- Dried pineapple, papaya or other fruits.

When you are weaning a flock of newly hatched chicks, consider the natural options as they will prevent the birds from getting used to pellets. They may not recognize pellets as food if they are not given any when you are weaning them.

If you bring birds home from a breeder or a pet store, chances are that their diet is mostly seed or pellet based. You can give them these foods mixed with natural foods. Then, slowly increase the proportion of natural foods. Eventually, you can remove seeds and pellets from the diet and only offer them as treats from time to time. The lesser you provide commercially packaged foods, the better it is for your bird.

Bird bread

You can prepare nutritious bird bread at home. Start with a muffin mix, preferably corn. Then, add eggs to this and blend them in. You can add several mashed vegetables to the mix. Run them all in a food processor to make a good batter for the cake.

When you want to give your bird some variety, you can even add blueberries, chopped nuts, raisins and fruits like apples after chopping them finely. The more variety you provide, the healthier the bird will be.

Bake this in a muffin pan to prepare the cake. Topping it with treats like cockatiel pellets will make the birds devour them in an instant. When you are baking the cake, bear in mind that you must not use any container that has Teflon coating. The fumes released by these pans can be extremely toxic to the birds.

This bread can be frozen and used on a regular basis. This is a quick fix when you do not have the time to make elaborate preparations for the bird.

Not only will the bird get all the nutrients that he needs, he will also enjoy the bread thoroughly.

Supplements
Supplementation should only be provided when you have consulted the avian vet. There are some safe options like cuttlebones that you can give your bird. These are usually treated like toys and the bird will enjoy chewing on them. That way, they will get a good source of calcium as well.

Another option for calcium supplementation is powdered calcium supplements that are prescribed by the vet. During the breeding season, you may have to switch to better options like the Cal Mag liquid with vitamin D. This will provide the birds with additional nutrients like Vitamin D and Magnesium that lead to a healthy clutch of eggs.

You can mix the supplements with the soft food as needed. It is best to start your bird off on the supplements about a week before the breeding season begins. When you are providing the bird with calcium during the breeding season, you will be able to avoid several problems related to the egg shell, such as breakage or improper development.

If you are adding any supplements to water, be sure to keep an eye on the bird. Sometimes, birds tend to dislike the taste and will stop consuming water altogether. Dehydration is the leading cause for illness and death in pet birds. If the supplement in water does not work for the bird, find alternate ways to administer it.

Water
If the nutrients must be absorbed into the system of your bird properly, he will need a constant supply of fresh water. Providing water in clean bowls is the best option. You must clean the water if you find any debris in it as it can become a breeding site for several micro-organisms that cause diseases.

Caiques love to bathe and you may occasionally find your bird dipping himself in the water bowl. If you notice this, consider providing him with two bowls. He will choose the one he wants to bathe in and the one he wants to drink from.

Foods you must avoid

There are certain foods that can be toxic to your bird. Make sure that the bird does not even accidentally gain access to any of the following foods:

- Avocadoes
- Coffee or anything containing caffeine
- Alcohol
- Pits of fruits
- Chocolate

Avoid dairy products altogether. However, if you must give your bird some ice cream, cheese or yoghurt, give it to them in very small quantities. Birds are lactose intolerant and may develop several digestive issues.

We always have the urge to give our birds some table scraps. While too much can cause obesity, it is not entirely wrong to share some of your food with your birds occasionally. Some foods that Caiques really enjoy are pasta, whole grain bread, rice, cooked vegetables, eggs and very well cooked lean meat.

Observe the eating habits of the bird. Knowing what he or she loves to eat can also help you provide him with the perfect treats when you begin to train them and want them to respond quickly.

2.Grooming

Keeping your bird clean is a must. The good news is that your Caiques need minimal grooming as they love to take a bath and preen themselves. If you can place a bird bath or an additional bowl of water, you will have a bird who will take a dip there from time to time.

There are a few grooming practices such as wing clipping and nail trimming that are mostly for the bird to stay safe in your home. You may have to give your bird a gentle bath at times if they get some debris on them or if they have any toxic substance on the body.

In order to groom your bird, the first step is to hand tame the bird. You should be comfortable handling your bird in order for these practices to be safe and to avoid any chance of injury.

Bathing a Caique

This usually does not take much effort. However, if you need to wash the bird for some reason such as any dirt or toxic substance on the body, you cannot really wait for him to get into the water voluntarily.

A shallow trough is the best option for a medium sized bird like the Caique. If the bird is hand tamed, you can hold him and lower him into the water legs first. If he squirms, hold still and when he settles down lower him more into the water.

Now, in case of a bird that is not hand tamed, place some spinach leaves or treats in the trough containing water. Then, take the trough to the door of the cage and let the bird walk into it.

A Caique will naturally take to water and will love to preen himself and get water all over him. Now, in case you have some sticky substance or debris, you can use a soft toothbrush to gently brush it off the body of the bird. If you can manage with just water, do so. However, in case of stubborn stains or substances, a very mild soap that has been diluted can be used. Make sure that you do not get any soap into the eyes or the nostrils of the bird.

Clipping the wings

Clipping the wings of the bird is a very controversial subject. Some pet owners are not comfortable with this practice. However, if your bird is going to spend a lot of time outside the cage, then wing clipping is a good idea to reduce his chances of getting away. If you are a first time owner, you may need some help to do this. It can be managed by you after you have observed your vet or an experienced Caique owner do it.

Follow these steps to effectively clip the wings of your bird:

- First, wrap the bird in a large towel when you take him out of the cage. Even if the bird is hand tamed, wing clipping is a new experience that may surprise your bird and make him a little nippy. Caiques are particularly known for being a little prone to biting. Hold him in a way that the ends of the towel go over your hands to offer protection.

- Place the bird on your lap or on a table. While the rest of the body is wrapped in the towel with one end on one hand, spread out one

52

wing of the bird. If the bird is moving around too much, wait for him to settle down before you proceed to clip the wing.

- The largest feathers are known as the primary feathers and are responsible for flight. You must clip the first two feathers, which are the largest. You may cut about 1 cm from each feather starting at the end. Repeat this process on the other side as well. Use a sharp pair of scissors so you can make the cut in one smooth motion.

- One thing you have to be certain about is symmetry. When you are done clipping both wings, spread them out and make sure that they are even. Now, any imbalance in the wings will make the bird unable to perch properly and will also have a hard time keeping his balance when walking.

- Sometimes, you may accidentally get a blood feather when you are clipping the wings. There will be a lot of bleeding but this is not something that you need to worry about. To prevent this from happening, watch the stem of the feather while you cut. The transparent part can be cut while the opaque part indicates the presence of capillaries.

- If you do get a blood feather, all you have to do is apply some styptic powder and provide light pressure on the area. It will solve the problem for you.

If you are unsure, you can get the wing clipped every six months at the vet. It will cost you about $15 or £10 every time. You may also practice with the vet before you do it yourself.

If a bird has clipped wings, it still does not mean that your bird is safe outside. The slightest wind can give your bird the lift and carry him off. This is one of the top causes for escapes among pet birds. Make sure that whenever you step outside you are keeping the bird in a carrier.

3.Maintaining the cage

The cage of the bird is where he is likely to spend most of his time. So it is important that you keep it clean and free from any chances of infection or contamination. There are daily, weekly and monthly checks that you must conduct mandatorily to keep the cage in its best condition.

Daily cleaning

When you feed your birds everyday, ensure that you check the cage thoroughly. Here are a few practices that are recommended for daily cleaning.

The food and water bowls

- Before you feed the bird, clean the bowls thoroughly. Rinse the bowls first and then lather them with soap. The soap must be washed off entirely. After the bowl is clean, towel it dry with a towel that is clean.

- Check if the dishes are dishwasher safe. In case you are planning to put them in the dishwasher, they must be suitable for it.

- The detergent that you use for cleaning must be animal safe. You can find several such options at the local pet store. If not, you will even be able to find them online or in stores that sell organic and natural products.

- It is always a good idea to have extra bowls for days when you may not have time to clean the bowls thoroughly.

Check the cage accessories

- Needless to say, you will have several perches and toys in the cage. If you notice that they have any dirt or droppings on them, you must clean them out thoroughly.

- The accessories are cleaned in the same manner as the dishes. Use animal friendly soap to lather up and then scrub them well. Using warm water is a good idea to disinfect these accessories a little better.

- When you put the toys back in the cage, you may want to move them around to give your bird some stimulation.

Cleaning the substrate or lining
- Replacing the cage lining material is a must. The best option available is paper lining available in stores or newspaper. These options are safe, easy to clean and economical.

- The old liner must be removed fully each day and the surface beneath it should be wiped with a rag or sponge to remove the paper that may be stuck on the floor.

- It is necessary that the lining material is free from any colored ink as these pigments can be toxic to your bird.

- The general rule is to have seven layers of paper at least. That way it is completely absorbent and you will have fewer pieces sticking to the floor.

When you are doing the daily cleaning, it is alright for the bird to stay in the cage. However, if you have had cases of the bird flying out of the cage, it is best that you keep him in a separate cage when you are doing so. You may use a travel carrier as a temporary option when you are cleaning the cage.

Weekly or monthly cleaning
You can set the schedule for cleaning the cage based on the number of birds that you have. The more the number of birds, the more often you have to clean. The size of the cage also matters. If the cage is smaller, it will have to be cleaned more frequently. With birds like Caiques that are medium sized, you can plan a fortnightly schedule as well as they are less likely to mess the cage up.

There are some simple steps that will help you be more organized when cleaning the cage:

- The first thing is to get all your supplies in place. You will need the following to clean your bird cage completely:
  - Cage liners
  - Cage wipes and paper towels

- Sandpaper
- Scrub brush or an old brush

Keep a garbage can handy to get rid of any debris or dirt in the cage.

- The bird must be kept in a safe cage or travel cage. It is best that you place the bird in alternate room in order to keep the fumes from the cleaning supplies away from the bird.

- All the toys and accessories must be removed from the cage.

- If you notice seeds on the floor or any loose droppings, get rid of them as well. The floor must be scrubbed hard with soapy water. Make sure that the soap is mild. It is also possible to place the cage in a large tub and then wash it with a hose. You can then spray the interiors with a disinfectant solution.

- Once you have washed the cage, it should dry completely before you place the accessories back. Air drying in the sun is the best option.

- The perches and toys should be cleaned completely to get rid of any debris or droppings. Rinse the accessories well before you apply any disinfectant on them. Some of these perches made from plastic or wood may also be safe to wash in the dishwasher. You can put the ropes and softer toys in the wash basin.

- The toys and accessories must be fully dried before they are placed back in. You can air dry them in the sun. If you do not have the time for it, you can even dry them in an oven.

- If you have two sets it is easier to manage the cage. Any toy or perch that is broken or frayed must be removed as it may lead to injuries.

- Once you have cleaned the cage, the next step is to clean the area around the cage. You may vacuum the area or even opt to wash and disinfect it. The area under the carpet should be cleaned fully too.

- Line the cage with new substrate, fill in fresh food and water and also put in all the dry items back into the cage.

It is also a good idea to clean the areas that the bird plays in, the travel cage to maintain complete hygiene with respect to the birds.

Knowing the disinfectants

Using safe disinfectants is just as important as cleaning the cage. You need to ensure that it is effective but at the same time is not harmful or toxic to your bird.

Birds are very sensitive to toxic fumes and you must choose very carefully. Here are a few tips about using disinfectants in the cage:

- The disinfectant must be potent enough to get rid of fungi, bacteria and viruses without harming the bird.

- There are many options available for you to choose at pet stores. However, the best option and most readily available one is household bleach. You can make a dilute solution of ½ cup of bleach in about a gallon of water.

- Remember that any organic material such as the seed or droppings must be removed completely before you use a disinfectant in the cage. They normally hinder the solution from working properly. The areas that have been soiled should be cleaned thoroughly with hot water mixed with a dishwashing solution. Then you can rinse in thoroughly before you spray the disinfectant.

- The disinfectant must be allowed to dry for at least ten minutes after it is applied onto a surface. Then you will rinse it with water. If you choose to use bleach solution, do so in an area that is well ventilated.

- Your safety is also very important and you must wear rubber gloves and safety goggles when you are cleaning the cage.

- The cage items must dry fully before placing it back. Any presence of moisture will make it a breeding ground for microbes.

If you are unsure about the disinfectant that you should use, you may ask your vet to provide you with the right options to clean the cage. In case of any health issue, the vet may provide you with medicated cage cleaners as well.

4.Travelling with the Caique

For birds, the most stressful thing can be travelling, even if it means a drive around the block. But, with vet visits and other requirements that will force you to take your bird for a drive means that you need a bird who is trained to remain calm in a car.

For birds, the biggest cause for stress is change. The more familiarity you try to bring when you are training your bird, the happier he will be. Now, the degree or the intensity of anxiety varies from one bird to another.

Some birds may just become comfortable on day one and for others it can mean several health issues and extreme anxiety. Here is a step-by-step process to help you make this easier for your bird:

- Get the bird a travel carrier. The first step is to get the bird used to this carrier. Make it a fun place by providing treats and toys every time the bird gets into this carrier without any sign of anxiety or fear. The best thing to do would be to open the door of the carrier and allow the bird to enter it on his own.

- Once the bird is entering the travel carrier, you can practice leaving him in there for a couple of hours. They are less likely to stress out while the carrier is still in the house, which has several familiar smells and sounds. You may even consider keeping the bird in the cage a few days before you actually have to take a long drive in the car.

- The next step is to introduce the bird to the car. Take the carrier and place it in the car for a few minutes and bring the bird back home. If the bird is stressed and shows signs of fluttering or even breathing with the beak open, take him back and try again till he is relaxing in the carrier when it is taken into the car.

- Then, you can drive around the block with the bird carrier in the backseat. A short five minute drive will help the bird get used to the movement. You do not have to make any elaborate preparations during this drive except lining the floor of the cage with a few extra layers of substrate.

- Now, the calmer you are, the calmer your bird is going to be. Stay relaxed when you are driving the bird. Avoid conversations, music and making too many noises when you are driving the bird.

- You may gradually increase the time that the bird spends in the moving car. For any trip that is longer than 15 minutes, make sure that you make enough water available. Using a bird water bottle is advisable when you are driving to avoid any spillage and dampness. The cage must be kept lined with enough substrate.

- Watch for signs of stress. The bird will keep the beak open, will retreat to a corner of the cage or will remain on the floor. The idea of being off balance is very stressful to the bird. With a moving car, this is one of the biggest issues. If the bird is getting very anxious, simply drive back home and put the bird in a quiet room. Do not try to verbally comfort your bird as it only causes more stress.

- When the bird is in the car, make sure that the windows are rolled up to prevent any drafts. You must keep the air conditioner on at room temperature. Since the bird is already under stress, temperature changes due to drafts or the air conditioner will only put the bird at risk.

- If you are going to be travelling with several bags, you might want to include them in the practice drives. The suitcases can be oddly shaped, too large or brightly colored. If the bird is caught off guard on the day of travel, your training efforts will just not pay off.

- If the travel period is longer than 20 minutes, take breaks to give your bird some food and water. While food is actually needed only twice a day, water is a must at regular intervals. Avoid treats and overfeeding when your bird is travelling, as it will make them sick.

- Birds are unable to poop when they do not have a steady perch. This is another reason why you must stop your car at regular intervals.

- Never take the carrier out of the car. There is always the slightest chance of the door being improperly shut and the bird getting away. It is a risk that you must never take when you are in the outdoors. It can become really challenging to find your Caique even though they are poor fliers. Even when the wings of the bird are clipped, the smallest breeze can give them the lift that they need to get away.

- You can even provide a sleeping tent or throw a blanket over half the carrier. That will give your bird a good place to retreat to incase he feels threatened or scared. They will also rest better when they have a cozy corner to cuddle up into.

- Watch out for signs of overheating and chilling. We will discuss this in the following chapters. Sometimes, the air-conditioner may be too cold or the exhaust fumes can lead to overheating in the bird. Provide the necessary first aid as mentioned in the following chapter.

Every time you travel by car with your bird, keep the car quiet. Sounding the horn, laughing, signing or talking loudly will be a stressor to the bird till he gets used to the car.

After the drive, take the bird home and let him relax in a quiet area of the house. Avoid forcing him to play, approaching him or talking to him for an hour or two. That is usually how long he will take to get over the ride and settle into his previous environment. Then he is fully stress free.

Travelling by air

There are times when you have to move or have to travel to a new city or country because of a job or some other commitment. Now, the challenging part is to take your pet bird with you. Especially since Caiques are considered exotic birds and are also listed under those that are endangered, you have to take care of several legal procedures as well.

If you are methodical and try to gather as much information as possible, it may not be so hard to manage travelling overseas with your bird. Here are the steps you will follow:

- Visit your vet. He is the best person to give you the information that you need about travelling with Caiques. You can visit the official website of the Convention on International Trade in Endangered Species or CITES to understand what permits you need. You will need to contact the US Fish and Wildlife Department or their contemporaries in your country. In some countries this process will take close to seven months so plan in advance.

- You will require a health certificate for your bird to travel with most airlines. The health certificate must be prepared as per the guidelines of the authorities of the country that you plan to travel to.

- Make a list of all the travel requirements of the major airlines. You must be sure that a certain airline that you choose allows birds to travel with them. You have to reserve a spot for your bird well in advance. This is because the number of pets allowed on board are limited in all airlines. Be sure to take a look at the pet policies of the airline that you choose in complete detail to avoid any last minute surprises or complications with respect to your bird's travel.

- You have to make sure that your bird has the right travel carrier. With airlines you have different requirements for in cabin use and cargo use. You must read about the dimensions and the weight of the carrier.

Make sure that the carrier is spacious enough for the bird. The bird must be able to stretch and flap his wings. There must be ample space to include the food and water bowls, a toy and a perch for the bird. To ease your bird's travel, make sure that he has ample space to perch. There are several airline approved bird carriers that you can purchase online.

It is best that you avoid any type of travel, by air or by road, during the summer months. In case you have to travel with your bird, make sure that you have reliable foster care. You can even hire a good pet sitter from a reputable agency. Make sure you conduct a lengthy interview in order to be sure of their experience with birds of this kind. Leave the bird's health records and the details of his vet with anyone who is taking care of your bird and make sure that you authorize at least one person to take health decisions for your bird when needed.

- Just like the transport carrier of your car, you need to make sure that the bird gets familiar with the airline carrier as well. You can ease the transition by letting him spend a few hours in the carrier everyday before you actually let him spend several hours in it.

The airline that you choose must be based on recommendations. Make sure that you ask around with other Caique or parrot owners to find one that is reliable and one that will handle the birds with care and even feed them and provide water in case of a long flight.

Chapter 5: Bonding with your Caique

Caiques form strong bonds with their families. However, there is always one person in the house whom he builds the strongest one with. Putting in some additional effort to spend time with your bird and training him will help you understand your bird better. Of course, it is a lot of fun when you find ways to interact with your bird.

It is also important to interact with your bird to check for any deviation from normal behavior, which may indicate underlying health issues. Playing with your bird and spending time training them is also wonderful stimulation for the mind of the bird.

1.Learning the body language

Birds communicate a lot with their body language. Understanding what the bird is indicating through this is the first step towards forming an unbreakable bond with him. Here are a few common signs that you need to learn to read to make your interactions with your bird more meaningful.

Your bird knows you

Caiques are extremely observant birds and will notice the slightest things about you. They recognize things like the hand that is used more often or is more dominant. This is one of the reasons why people often notice that certain birds will only step on to the right or left hand, for instance.

Through their observations, birds will be able to tell which hand is used more often. This is the hand that is steadier when the bird steps on it, perhaps. There are several cases when a bird accustomed to a right hand will refuse to step up when someone offers their left hand.

This is true even for petting. If the hand that you normally use to pet the bird is the right one, he may back away from a right hand when he doesn't want to be pet.

These are a few examples that help you understand that several conceived behavioral issues are actually just the result of conditioning. That is why, when you interact with your bird, you need to be aware of everything from your posture to the hand that you use when you approach your bird.

Learning about parrot postures
The way your bird stands can tell you a lot about the state of mind that is in. For instance:

- If the bird is standing upright and the feathers are smooth or pulled in, the bird is being cautious or is afraid.

- If the bird is upright but the feathers look loose and relaxed, he is happy and calm.

- When the bird is perched on one foot and has the feathers puffed out, he may either be cold or may be unwell.

- A bird whose feathers have been stretched away from the body while the wings are held out is getting ready to fight or is courting a female.

Birds show warning signs
Before they reach in and bite a person, Caiques will give you three important signals. When you do see these signs, you need to stay clear of the bird or simply put him back in the cage. If you can find a toy in the vicinity, offer it to the bird to ensure that he is actually going for it and is not getting ready to land a powerful bite on your finger. Here are five signs that you must look out for:

- The bird looks around to get a good aim at the object that he wants to bite.

- The beak will be open when he is looking for the object.

- He will widen his stance and will get a firm grip on the perch or will charge at the object that he wants to bite.

- The bird will emit a purring sound that shows a sign of either irritation or contentment. Take a look at the body language of the bird when he is purring.

- Growling is a type of vocalization that indicates aggression beyond doubt. In fact this is rarely seen in pet birds. If your bird does exhibit this, he is either being bothered by something or does not want to be pet by you.

Knowing that your bird is happy
Even when a bird is relaxed and happy, he will give you some signals:

- Birds will do a happy dance. This will involve extended motions of the wing and the leg on one side of the body and then bringing them back before doing the same with the other side.

- The bird will stretch the feathers completely to the side or will hold them up while returning them against the back. He will repeat this several times when he is happy. This is when he sees his human approaching or when you offer a toy or treat.

- The bird will wag his tail and will move it back and forth as if he is shaking water off the surface. This is an indication that the bird is happy and is looking forward to more such occurrences. He will usually display this behavior when he is all ready to play.

- If you ever fear that your may have had an unpleasant experience such as forceful handling, remove the bird from that situation and put him back on the perch. If he wags his tail, then he is happy. But if you see that he does not display any signs of joy such as wagging the tail or puffing the feathers, it may have been a stressful experience for me.

- The bird will wiggle his tongue or will move the beak up and down to indicate happiness.

- They will lower the head with the feathers just about the beak fanned out indicating that they want you to pet them.

- Caiques are known for turning the head upside down or lying on their back when they are happy.

- Whistling and singing indicate a bird that is very happy and content.

- They will click their tongue when they are excited and want you to play with them.

- A happy bird will murmur or chatter softly when he is resting.

When your bird is excited
When there is adequate stimulation in the environment, birds show signs of being motivated towards it. These are either related to play or courtship. When it is the latter, there are more chances of your bird being aggressive and it is best that you stay away from your bird during these times.

- Caiques and other parrots show a unique sign of stimulation, which is called pinpointing. This is when the pupil contracts making the colored part of the eye or the iris look much larger than it normally is. This indicates a motivation to either play, bite or mate. You must watch the body language of the bird to decipher flashing or pinpointing.

- If your bird is walking with the wings flared and the eyes pinpointed with occasional flapping of the wings, it is a clear sign that the bird is ready to breed. He will show you other signs such as keeping the wings out and shifting his body weight from side to side.

Caiques can be tricky
Caiques know how to manipulate their humans. In fact, in many cases, these birds will find it amusing when they trick you using their body language. Now this can lead to unpleasant experiences for you and it is your duty as a pet owner to warn anyone who approaches the bird.

- The bird will appear to be friendly and inviting and will go straight for the hand or the finger.

- Fake stabbing is also a common behavior with Caiques. They almost try to test any new person approaching them by gently poking the finger or hand with the beak. When the person jumps away, it is a win for the bird!

- This behavior must be managed to prevent any untoward incidents related to the bird.

- When you do not stop this behavior in your Caique, it will become more frequent as the birds really think of it as play and fun.

The satisfaction of a content bird
In the end what every pet owner wants is for their Caique to be happy and content. If you are able to give your bird a good home and a healthy environment to thrive in, you will notice these signs in him:

- When the bird is sleeping, he will hold one foot up and will pull in all the feathers.

- The feathers just above the beak are flared.

- The bird will grind his teeth while keeping the eyes partially closed or fully closed.

The more the body language indicates happiness and contentment in the bird, the better it is. This shows that the bird is responding well to any training that you may be providing and that he is in the best of health.

On the other hand, regular signs of aggression or several warning signs indicate that your bird is being bothered by something. Checking the environment and removing possible stressors will work. If not, you may even consider getting your bird checked by a vet.

2.Training your Caique

Investing time on training your Caique gives you a bird that is more social and a lot easier to handle. Some forms of training such as hand training are important for your safety while others like step up can be very useful in getting your bird out of possibly unpleasant situations.

Caiques are very responsive to training. Teaching them new tricks is also quite easy. This time that you spend training your bird is mentally stimulating for the bird and can be a great way for you to bond with your bird.

Hand-taming

Normally, breeders will hand tame the bird before they are sold. However, if you have had hatchlings at home or have a young bird who has not been hand tamed, this is the most important type of training that your bird will need. It will help you make your interactions with your bird more peaceful.

- Start off by helping the bird get used to your hand. Place the hands on the sides of the cage and watch the bird's body language. Continue to do this until the bird is calm and not visibly uncomfortable with your hand being there.

- Then, open the door of the cage and place your hand inside. The bird may flutter and move away or may just be calm. If the bird seems unsettled, hold your hand in calmly and watch out for the warning signs of biting. If you see none, keep your hand there till the bird settles down. Then, retreat and stop the training. Do this a couple of times until the bird is not disturbed with your hand being in the cage.

- When you are changing the water and food bowls in the morning, try to offer a few pellets or a piece of fruit on your palm to the bird before replacing the bowls. Some birds will readily take the food while others will hesitate. Even if it takes a few attempts, be consistent. You can approach the bird gently if he is hesitant.

- Once the bird has become used to eating from your palm, you can try to give him a treat using your index finger and thumb. Hold the food out to the bird with two fingers and let him eat from it.

Holding your hand like a perch will help him in the next step of training.

- Eventually, your bird will come to you on his own when you hold the food out. You can be sure that he has formed a positive association with your hand when he moves towards it, even if you are not holding a treat in your hand.

- When you are hand taming your bird, make sure that you sit down and stay at his eye level so that he does not feel threatened. Towering over the cage will put you in a predatory position that will definitely make your bird uncomfortable.

- Never catch your bird by surprise if he is not fully hand tamed. Approaching the bird when he is resting, or making too many sudden movements will definitely make your bird weary of your hand. That will defeat the entire purpose of hand taming.

- One thing you must never do is grab the bird without hand taming him first. This will leave a long lasting negative impression on his mind and will make him lose trust. Ease your way in when you are hand taming your bird or when you are trying to get your bird to settle in.

- When your bird is comfortable in your home, you can move the cage to a busier part of your home. That way, the bird gets to observe you and your family and will eventually understand that you are his flock now.

- If your bird does escape during a training session, never grab him. Instead, put a towel over him and then hold him with the towel wrapped around when you are putting him back in the cage.

If you have a pair of birds, then they will have an extremely strong bond with one another. This will make it slightly harder to hand tame the bird as they are not really looking for any interaction outside the cage. However, you can achieve great results when you tame one bird at a time.

The more relaxed and happy your bird is, the more positive will your training sessions be. Keeping the cage clean, providing toys and good food are the foundation to great training sessions.

Step up training

Getting your bird to step up on your finger can be very important to take care of your bird. In case your bird is in an unpleasant situation such as an attack by a predator or if the bird is exposed to any fumes.

Step up training is the next step after you have hand tamed your bird. Using a target is the best option when it comes to step up training. Get your bird to follow a target on to your finger. The target can be a fruit or treat that you hold in the other hand while you are trying to get him to step up on one hand. It can also be a stick with a treat at the end of it that the bird can follow.

Begin with an artificial perch such as one made of wood if you are not comfortable with the bird perching on your finger. Hold the treat behind the perch and wait for the bird to step up on to it. Only when the bird has both his feet secured on the perch will you give him the treat.

It is best that you use a training perch when you are trying to establish trust with the bird. One thing that a bird will easily lose trust on is a shaky perch. It makes them very uncomfortable.

In fact, you will notice that the bird will bite or check the perch with his beak before stepping on to it. If you are offering your finger as a perch, be prepared for the bird to hold it with the beak before he steps on it. He is not trying to bite you but is only making sure that it is a steady perch.

If you withdraw the hand when he does this, chances are that you will have to work really hard to re-gain the trust of your bird.

When you offer the perch to the bird, use a cue word such as "Step-up" or "Up". Once the bird actually steps up, you can offer him a treat. After the treat is given, let the bird get back into the cage. Once he steps off, offer another treat or toy and end the training.

Offering the treat after the bird steps off tells the bird that going back to the cage is also a good thing. This helps when the bird forms a bond with you. In most cases, leaving their human and going back into the cage is a very stressful experience for birds. If you train them to learn that the cage is a positive space from the beginning, they will not feel stressed when you put them back

Eventually, the bird will respond to the verbal cue without any treat. Once the bird perches on your finger comfortably, you can use the same technique to lead the bird to perch on your shoulder or your head as well.

Potty Training

If you plan to leave your bird out of the cage, the last thing you want is to have bird poop all over your furniture or clothes. Most people are comfortably able to get parrots to perch on their shoulder and carry out chores at home. When the bird is spending a lot of time outside his enclosure, you need to learn to house break them or train them to poop where you want them to.

The good news is that Caiques respond to this training quite well. Of course, you need to be committed and you must reinforce any behavior that is positive.

Observation of parrot behavior in the wild has revealed that they usually defecate in one place as a survival tactic. The less they leave a trail, the lesser they are prone to predator attacks. In fact, hens that are brooding will not leave the nest all night. Parrots will seldom poop at night and will usually have a large poop in the morning.

This behavior shows us that they are conscious and are quite aware of where they should defecate and when they should do so. You can use this behavior to your advantage and potty train the bird. Any parrot can learn this behavior but the younger the better.

There are three simple steps to teaching your bird where to poop:

Observe their pattern

The feeding pattern and the age plays a very important role in training. For instance, baby birds that are being raised on formula will poop every twenty minutes. Older birds will usually poop every twenty minutes. The time gap can increase up to eight hours in some cases.

Make it a point to observe the pattern of your bird's poop and the frequency. The time of the day and the interval between eating and pooping are important notes for you to take.

Praise each poop
Let your bird stay in the cage or on a perch. When he poop praise him verbally using a word that you want him to associate with pooping. For instance "Good poop" is commonly used. The bird will obviously not understand this in the first go. Be consistent.

Indicate the place to poop in
When you take the bird out of the cage, be aware of the frequency and put him back in the cage to prevent accidents. The half time principle works best. For example, if the bird poops every twenty minutes, put him back within ten minutes of getting him out of the cage.

When he poops, praise him again with the verbal command.

If you are consistent with this process, Caiques are known to get potty trained in about 72 hours. If the bird takes longer, you need to be more persistent. You will actually see the bird getting into position to poop when you approach the cage. This is his eagerness to get out of the cage and be with you. When this happens frequently, you will be able to get your bird to poop with the verbal command.

While a bird can be trained to poop on command, you cannot really control the bowel movement initially. When you are sure that the bird can poop on command, you can teach him to hold it till you find an appropriate place to defecate.

When birds are about to poop, they will lower the rump and lift the tail up. It almost seems like he is doing a push up. You can give the command "No" and gently push the tail down. Then, take him to the cage or any other place that you think is appropriate to poop in.

If he poops in the right place, praise and reward good behavior. If the bird has an accident, do not react. Just clean up and wait for your next opportunity to correct the behavior.

Never startle your bird when you are trying to teach him something new. Running to the place that you want him to poop or shouting at him will not help him learn. They do not want to have the accident. The only thing you must do is provide positive reinforcement every time good behavior is displayed.

For younger birds, gaining control over bowel movements is harder, just like a human baby. Ideally when they are about one year old, they should be able to master control. If you are unable to stop the bird before he defecates, do not reprimand him. He will not even associate the negative reinforcement with his behavior. He is probably thinking about how fun it is to play with you and you are pushing him away with a scold. That will only leave him confused.

There is a common myth that teaching the bird to poop on command may lead to instances when the bird holds it in for so long that he dies. This is not true and has never occurred. If fact, just like humans, bowel control is a natural process for birds. In the wild, it is necessary for the bird to mark the boundaries of the territory. If they are out foraging, they will only poop when they come back to their "spot".

Potty training allows the bird to socialize more. You will not have to worry about things like your bird pooping on the shoulders of guests or in someone else's home. This will actually help your relationship with the bird in the long run.

3.Dealing with behavioral issues
Socialization of birds is limited to their ability to behave well. They usually develop issues that are the result of our interaction with them. When we accidentally reinforce wrong behavior or when we act irresponsibly by grabbing the bird or teasing him, he may develop these issues.

Now, with Caiques, they already have a reputation of being very nippy. The issue may escalate if not controlled early. They also develop problems like screeching when you leave the room. This will turn your experience with the bird sour. Behavioral issues are the number one reason for birds being abandoned.

Caique bite prevention
Caiques have a reputation for being biters. There are many instances when the owner is unable to control the behavior leading to sharp and painful bites. That said, it is possible to teach your bird that biting is

not good behavior. For starters, you must understand what makes your bird bite and remove the stimulus to see a notable change.

Why Caiques bite

There are several things that will make your Caique react by nipping your hand. Here are a few common causes for biting:

- The way you approach your bird is very important. If you are feeling anxious or nervous, it is not a good idea to pick the bird up or approach him. That will induce bad behavior in the bird, as they are very sensitive to how we are feeling. They do not really think about biting and will only do it as a reflex.

- The bird may have learnt to associate your hands with something negative. When you use your hands to punish the bird by shoo-ing them away or by throwing something at them, they will learn to react by biting. The best way to stop your bird from doing something is to redirect the attention with a toy.

- You use your hands only when you are taking the bird in and out of the cage. Sometimes, when the bird is not calm, they may make the association of the hand with unwanted touching or petting. Try other options like perches and play with the bird when he is out on a perch. Even when you pick the bird up, you may want to walk around or do something fun that makes the bird think of your hand as a positive thing.

- The bird may be reacting to defend himself. If you have adopted a bird, he may have had a history of being beaten or threatened. Even when you make sudden movements with your hands and startle the bird, you will stimulate him to bite you.

- When you are approaching your bird, do it gently and without any jerks. The calmer you are and the more used to your hand the bird gets, the more he will respond to your hand positively. When the bird gains trust, you will notice that his nipping transforms into a more playful one as opposed to one that is very forceful.

74

- Putting the bird back in the cage is stressful for him and the bite may be a sign of protest when he does not want to go back in. You can make this more pleasant by putting some of your bird's favorite food in the cage before putting him back. Engaging in play or walking around before putting him back will also help. The less predictable you make this, the easier it is for you and your bird.

- Putting your bird back in the cage as punishment is the worst thing you can do. Then the cage becomes a place that the bird does not want to go into. Then, he will learn to fight you every time you try to put him back.

- Sometimes, a bird will hold your finger with his beak as a form of play. This is not painful. However, when you try to free your finger, the bird may dig the deep in more. The best way to release your finger is to hold the bird with the other hand and pull him away gently. You can even redirect the bird using a toy or a perch that he may like to chew.

- Birds can become territorial at times leading to this behavior. This may require you to change your approach to your bird a little. Try to get a cage that will allow you to change food and water bowls from the outside. You must also let the bird come out of the space using a target before you handle him. That way he is in a neutral territory and is less likely to bite.

- Your bird may be hormonal and may begin to bite people whom he perceives as competition. Then you can reduce the interaction of that person with the bird. You can even ask your vet for medicines to balance the hormones if you do not intend to breed your bird. Limiting daylight hours can also help you manage hormone related biting.

Preventing bites

As discussed in the previous section, your bird will give you signs when he is about to bite. Understanding your bird's body language will help you retreat in time before you are bitten. If someone else is handling your Caique or is playing with him, you can take the bird away when he shows the signs of biting.

The best way to prevent biting is to hand tame your bird. This will help your bird trust you more and will reduce nipping overtime. When you are interacting with the bird, stay calm. You must approach them gently and even keep your talking voice low when interacting with the bird.

Understand the personality of your bird. While humans love to cuddle and play, some birds may not really be fond of it. If your Caique has shown you signs that he needs his space, respect that and find other ways to interact with your bird. That way, he is less stressed and will be calmer.

Teaching your bird not to bite
It is possible to train your Caique not to bite. There are three things that you can do:

- When your bird bites, push the beak down gently or just blow in the bird's face. This is a little uncomfortable for the bird and he will reduce biting when you do this often.

- If the bird is on your hand when he bites, just shake your hand. You can run if the bird is on your shoulder. This is a great way to make the bird lose focus and release the grip on your finger. In addition to that, being on a shaky perch is very uncomfortable for birds and they will immediately learn that biting is not a good thing.

- Putting the bird on the floor will make them less aggressive as this is a new territory that makes them feel vulnerable.

When your bird bites, you will reinforce the behavior by pulling away or shouting. It is a better idea to actually push your hand or finger towards the bird to make them release the grip. Pulling away is the reaction that your bird is hoping for and when you do the opposite you actually surprise them.

Caique separation anxiety

Separation anxiety in Caiques can be heartbreaking and frustrating at the same time. If your bird is crying out in distress every time you leave the room, he may have developed separation anxiety. It is actually very stressful for a bird to be away from the human that he has bonded with. And when you feel sorry for your bird, you actually feed into this behavior that can be stressful for you, the bird and the people around you.

The first thing that you need to do is to stop trying to calm your bird down. Even a reprimand such as "No" or "Stop" is reinforcement for the bird. He thinks of it as a response to the call. You must get out of his sight and reward him when he is quiet. Even if he is able to stop screeching for a few minutes, return and reward the bird.

Distracting your bird will also help prevent separation anxiety. When your bird is engaged in something else, he will completely forget that you even left the room.

Just before you are about to leave, place a foraging toy in the cage. You can even scrunch up a paper with treats and leave it in the cage. Leaving a window open is also a good idea as it will give your bird something to watch or will offer ample distraction when you are away. It will also teach the bird that being alone and independent is quite a good thing actually.

Make the ritual of leaving really calm. Avoid any interaction with your bird for at least half an hour before you leave initially. You will be able to reduce this time as your bird gets more used to being on his own. Saying bye to your bird or waving at him will make him anxious. The best thing to do is to leave calmly when you bird is settled in.

Give your bird good physical exercise with toys. You also have to provide your bird with ample mental stimulation. When your bird's energy is all drained out, he is less likely to screech for long periods of time. They will want to rest and will do so even if you are away.

If you are unable to work on the behavior issues on your own, you may consult your vet or can look for a bird trainer who will be able to provide you with tips. Dealing with behavioral issues is the key to building a good relationship with your bird.

Remember that they will be with you for close to four decades and you will not be able to put up with bad behavior for too long.

Chapter 6: Breeding Caiques

In captivity, Caiques do not breed as readily as other species of parrots. Usually, they begin to breed only when they are about 2 years old. It is recommended that you encourage breeding when they are 3 years old to ensure better health of the clutch.

1.The breeding season

The breeding season depends upon the climate in the area that they live in. Birds that live in the northern hemisphere usually begin to breed around late November until June. In the southern hemisphere breeding seems to be more erratic and can occur at any time of the year.

You will notice significant changes in the bird's behavior. The male tends to become aggressive and may even cause harm to the female which requires you to keep an eye out. The hen will begin to build the nest and will start collecting small items for the cage.

The male will chase the hen around the cage and may, in rare cases, kill the hen because of his aggressive behavior. The male is frantic to mate, as he needs to ensure that the eggs are fertile. Usually mating takes place 48 hours before the eggs are laid.

Caiques will breed even if other pairs are present in the cage, quite unlike most parrot species. They will usually choose the same mate every breeding season. When the female is ready to lay the egg, her abdomen becomes large. In some cases, the bird may not lay the eggs for several weeks after mating. If you are worried about egg binding, you may consult the vet.

2.Pairing Caiques

The first step is to determine whether you have a true pair. Do not take the word of the breeder or the pet store when it comes to the gender of the bird. With Caiques, the best method to determine the gender is through DNA sexing. It is an inexpensive process that will help you create pairs faster.

When the birds are of the breeding age, they are most likely to accept a partner. However, if you are trying to introduce and older bird who has had a mate previously, it is a lot harder.

Never introduce the bird during the breeding season, as they tend to be more aggressive during this time. Do it a few months before. The first step is to place the bird in separate cages and place them side-by-side.

If there is no resistance, you can let both the birds out of the cage and allow them to interact in a neutral space under supervision. If the birds are calm and comfortable, you can place them in a cage together. Put them in a cage that is new to both of them to prevent any territorial behavior.

If you have to use an old cage, you must place the female inside before you introduce the male. You know that there is pair bonding between the birds if they sleep in the same nest box, sit on the perch together and preen each other. They may have spats once in a while. As long as it is not potentially dangerous, there is no need for you to interfere, as this behavior is quite normal for Caiques.

3.Preparing for breeding
The cage needs to be prepared for Caiques to be able to breed properly. It is a good idea to give them a separate cage which is enough to accommodate one pair. A smaller cage than the regular one can be used.

The good thing about Caiques is that they do not require a fancy nesting box. Any size and shape is good enough for them as long as the pair can fit in comfortably. You can use an elongated cardboard box that measures about 10 inches in depth and height and about 24 inches in length. Using boxes that have an internal shelf can help you with your Caiques. As these birds tend to push out most of the bedding when they are about to lay eggs, you will have to provide them with new bedding every time. With an internal shelf type nesting box, the bedding will collect in the bottom and you can just replace it as long as it is clean.

It is best that you provide your bird with lot of natural light. If that is not possible, then you can use a fluorescent light. Full spectrum lights can be placed near the cage, to give the bird about 13 hours of daylight. If the light is provided for longer, the birds will breed all year long.

Position the breeding cage against the wall in a quiet area. This will give your bird a sense of security. When they are against the wall, they know that they will not have any threat from that side.

4. Nutrition

Your birds will need a lot of good food to lay healthy and fertile eggs. A balanced meal that contains about 35% fresh produce, 20% seed and 45% formulated pellets is the best option.

Try to give your Caique more fruits in comparison to vegetables in this season. As they prefer sweet foods, they will consume them more readily.

One of the most important nutrients for Caiques in this season is amino acids. They are available from foods like meat, which is not really the natural diet for the bird. That is why you need to give them a vet recommended formulated pellet diet. A piece of yellow cheese or eggs can also help your bird. Additional protein is required when the bird is entering the breeding season. Your vet may recommend larvae, which is available in pet stores.

Calcium is another essential nutrient to ensure that the eggs are synthesized properly. You will notice that females will begin to compulsively chew on objects that provide a source of minerals. Giving your bird cuttlebone is a good idea. The mineral blocks that are available in pet stores are usually rejected by Caiques. If the bird does not get enough calcium, she will chew on plaster on the walls and even on brick surfaces.

If the bird is ignoring cuttlebones as well, you can give them an oyster shell. Calcium supplements can also be recommended by the vet.

5. Egg laying and incubation

Normally, a clutch will consist of about 4 eggs. They are medium sized white eggs. The first egg of the clutch is the largest one and the size seems to decrease eventually. The eggs are laid at an interval of two to three days.

The incubation period is usually 26 days but may vary slightly. One common issue with Caique hens is that they do not sit very tight on the clutch. That may require you to provide an electric heater below the nesting box at a temperature of about 75 degree F.

The eggs hatch in the order that they have been laid. You will have to check the chicks after the first feed. They should be huddled up and must be warm when you touch them. If one of the chicks is cold when you touch him or is away from the others, it might indicate that the parents are neglecting him. In many cases, the parent will only feed one or two chicks that hatched first and will neglect the other. You will have to remove this bird from the clutch and hand feed him.

The best practice is to co-parent the chicks. This means that you will have to allow the parents to feed the ones that you leave with them while handling them at least once each day. Be stealthy about picking up the chicks though. The parents will start plucking the chick if they are not comfortable with you handling them. Chicks must only be handled when they open their eyes.

When the parents are out of sight, you can use a treat to lure him to you and then pick him up. Handling a chick is not very important when the bird has fledged or developed flight feathers.

6. Hand feeding

Hand feeding is one of the best ways to tame the chicks. You can choose to hand feed all of them when they are a few days old. That is when you will transfer them to an incubator at 95 degree F. After the first week, the temperature should be dropped by about three degrees.

The chicks should have enough warmth to be able to digest the food that you provide them. If the birds feel cool when you touch them, increase the temperature slightly. If they seem red or keep their wings away from the body, reduce the temperature.

It is quite easy to handfeed Caique chicks. You can use commercially available formula to hand feed them. Use a small syringe or ink dropper to feed the chicks. Make sure that you weigh the chicks every day. They will gain weight each day as they are growing.

When they are very young, you can feed them every three hours. The time can be increased as they grow. Never feed the bird in the middle of the night. The first feed should be at about 6 AM and the last one at about 11 PM.

The food should not be more than 105 degree F in temperature. This may burn the crop of the bird. If it is too cold, the birds will not eat the food at all.

Weaning is quite simple with Caiques, given their curious nature. You can place a few pieces of sliced grapes when they begin to pick at objects. Then, you can add foods like spray millet or safflower seeds. When they begin to eat this, you can give them more varieties of foods. When chicks are reared in groups, they will wean faster than those raised alone.

7. Developmental issues

There are a few developmental issues that you may notice with the hatchlings within the first few days. The most common issues are:

- Spraddled leg or spayed legs: To prevent this, you can keep the young birds in a small bowl so that the legs stay right under their body. They must not be placed on smooth surfaces that do not provide them with enough grip. Feed the birds when they are standing on some surface like paper to give them good support. If the condition is very severe you will have to use surgical tape to hold the legs closer to each other.
- Misdirected toe: This is a toe that will not point in the direction that is normal. For parrots it is common to have two toes pointing forward and two back. However, in some cases, they may be born with three toes pointing forward. In the first few days, the toe will turn backwards on its own. If this does not happen properly, then you will have to tape the toe to the one that is facing in the right direction for about a week. Eventually, it will stay in the right position.

- Constricted toe: This is when the skin on the toe becomes very tight and prevents blood flow. This requires a trip to the vet to have it surgically corrected.

Developmental issues are often the result of improper nutrition. So you need to make sure that you do not compromise on your bird's diet.

Chapter 7: Health Problems in Caiques

Like most species, there are a few health issues that are common with Caiques. In this chapter, we will discuss everything from identifying a sick bird, the common illnesses and proper precautions to make sure that your bird is in the best of health.

As the bird owner, the bird's health is your top priority. You must ensure that your bird is checked every year even if he seems to be in perfectly good health. That is when you will be able to identify problems in the initial stages and deal with them, if any.

1. Identifying a sick bird

The first step towards knowing if your bird needs any medical attention is to be able to identify if he is healthy or not. There are some signs that you will see when the bird's health is deteriorating. Keep an eye out for the slightest change in the bird's normal behavior. If the symptoms are severe, it also means that the infection or health issue is severe.

The earlier you catch the condition, the higher are the chances of your bird getting medical attention before the issue is permanent or irreversible. These are the signs you must watch out for:

- The beak develops spots or abnormalities. If the beak is dry and is peeling or has any discharge, it is an indication of health issues.

- The bird is bleeding.

- Breathing is very difficult and strained.

- The bird lets out sharp coughs.

- Drooling is a common sign of yeast infection.

- The eyes of the bird seem to be red, swollen or runny.

- The skin seems to be itchy or sore. The bird may have bald patches or abnormal falling of feathers even when it is not the molting season.

- The bird is plucking out his own feathers.

- The position of the head is abnormal. This may manifest in the form of circling of the head or twisting that seems unusual. The head may even twitch or shake in some cases.

- The head has wet feathers and seem soiled. This is a sign that the bird has been vomiting, especially if the wetness is restricted to the head.

- The joints of the bird seem to be swollen and the bird is less mobile or is hesitating to stand up.

- The legs seem weak or may even be paralyzed.

- The droppings have more urine or have an abnormal color or consistency.

- The bird experiences seizures from time to time.

- The vent or the cloaca of the bird is swollen or has some soreness around it.

- The crop or the abdomen of the bird is extremely swollen.

- There are lumps or tumors on the body.

- The bird seems to have lost his voice or the voice of the bird shows sudden changes.

- The wings are drooping.

- The bird shows sudden fluctuations in his weight.

- Vomiting is a common sign of illness. Regurgitation is a common behavior in parrots. When the bird regurgitates, the undigested food is thrown out. If there is not food particle in the expulsion, it might indicate vomiting.

- The bird is refusing to leave the floor of the cage.

- The bird seems to be lethargic and uninterested in the toys.

- Food consumption reduces drastically or increases significantly.

- The bird may consume excess water or may not drink water at all.

With these signs, you can be sure that your bird needs medical attention. When neglected, the issue will escalate, often leading to sudden death in the bird. The more you interact with your birds, the more likely you are to observe even the smallest drift from normalcy.

2. Common health issues with Caiques

There are a few health issues that you will find common to most of the new world parrots. Unfortunately, most of these conditions manifest late and put the bird at the risk of permanent damage and in severe cases, death. Make sure that you learn in as much detail about these conditions as possible to prevent them and also to identify the possibility of your bird developing the condition.

This section lists all the causes, symptoms, diagnosis methods and the outcome of the condition or the prognosis of each condition that is likely to affect Caique parrots.

Aspergillosis

Transmission

- The condition is transmitted by a type of mold called *Aspergillusfumigatus*.
- It is a condition that humans may contract as well.
- It is usually transmitted from the parent to the chick.
- If the concentration of the mold is too high in the air, the water or the food, the birds may be infected.

- It is also transmitted in cages that are over-crowded.

Symptoms:
- Labored breathing
- Inability to vocalize or rasping when the bird tries to vocalize
- Anorexia
- Depression
- Loss of control on bodily movements
- Nasal discharge
- Lesions in the eyes
- Inflammation of the eyes

Diagnosis
- Polymerase chain reaction test
- Anti-body titer

Prognosis
- The condition leads to complications in the respiratory system.
- The mold may colonize in several organs of the body leading to organ or tissue damage.
- Nebulization is an option to control the condition.
- It may lead to death in most cases, as the infection can be severe.

Avian flu or influenza

Transmission:
- The condition is transmitted from the infected bird through the water, food, nasal or oral discharge.
- Hardy viruses may be present when the temperature is not properly controlled. The lower the temperature, the higher the chances of contracting this condition.
- Although there are few recorded cases, this condition may affect human beings as well.

Symptoms:
- Depression
- Lethargy
- Loss of limb control

- Loss of appetite
- Inability to stand or walk
- Staying close to the floor of the cage
- Labored breathing
- The bird is unable to stay stable on a perch

Diagnosis:
- Usually this condition leads to death in the birds and the diagnosis only occurs when the body of the bird is examined through a necropsy.

Prognosis:
- There is very little you can do if the bird is diagnosed with this condition. It is 100% fatal in most cases.

Avian tuberculosis

Transmission:
- It is caused by a type of bacteria called *mycobacterium avium*.
- It is generally transmitted through the feces.
- It can also be transmitted from contaminated food or water.
- Some birds may be carriers of the condition and an increased concentration of the pathogen in the environment leads to infections.

Symptoms:
- The birds develop a lumpy mass under the skin
- Chronic wasting is seen
- Diarrhea
- Swollen joints
- Lameness
- Depression

Diagnosis
- Microscopic examination of the lab cultures
- Biopsy
- Endoscopy

Prognosis
- The condition is very common in birds that are housed outdoors or when they are imported.
- Strict isolation or quarantining is one of the best ways to treat the condition.

Chlamydiosis or parrot fever

Transmission
- The condition is transmitted by a microorganism called *Chlamydiophilapsittaci.*
- It is transmitted through any discharge from the eye or the nasal area.
- This organism is very hardy and has the ability to survive in any dried feces of in the environment in many forms.
- This microorganism is a threat to human beings and can cause severe infections.

Symptoms:
- Labored breathing
- Loss of appetite
- Depression
- Lethargy
- Diarrhea
- Sudden weight loss
- Yellow or green droppings
- Nasal discharge
- Discharge from the eyes

Diagnosis

- PCR tests
- Blood tests
- Cloacal swab test
- Observation of a laboratory culture of the microorganism

Prognosis

- Usually the bird will recover from the condition when it is detected early.
- A six week cycle of doxycycline is recommended
- Preventive measures are a must, as repeated infection will lead to respiratory problems that can be permanent.

Glardiasis

Transmission
- The microorganism responsible for this condition is present in the feces.
- It can also be transmitted through food or water that is contaminated.
- Glardiasis can be transmitted from the bird to humans.

Symptoms
- Feather plucking
- Sudden weight loss
- Bright yellow or green colored urates
- Nutritional deficiency
- Diarrhea

Diagnosis
- There are several tests that are available but this condition is not detected reliably.
- In most cases, the response to the treatment is the only way to diagnose the condition.

Prognosis
- The response to this treatment is usually very good.
- Treatment can be prolonged if the bird is still showing symptoms and if there is a chance of a bird being a carrier.
- The entire flock must be treated to prevent repeated infection.
- Medication like metronidazole and rhonidazole are recommended for effective management of the condition.
- Immune support is provided in the form of a good diet and exercise.

Newcastle's Disease

Transmission
- This condition is normally transmitted through the feces.
- Other sources of infection include nasal discharge, ocular discharge, contaminated food or water.
- The pathogen is quite hardy and can be present in the environment for several days in the presence of the right conditions.
- This is another disease that may affect human beings as well.

Symptoms:
- Usually there are no signs in the initial stages. The symptoms occur only after the bird is severely infected.
- Depression
- Paralysis
- Dyspnea
- Loss of appetite
- Weight loss
- Impairment of neurological function

Diagnosis
- In most cases the condition is diagnosed only when the body of a bird is inspected after death.

Prognosis
- For most parrot species, chances of recovery are poor.
- Even when the bird does recover, he could be a carrier of the condition.
- Usually, the bird dies before the condition can be managed.

Psittacine beak and feather disease

Transmission
- Infection is caused by *PsittacineCircovirus* 1 or *PsittacineCircovirus 2.*
- It is usually transmitted through feather dander, blood or feces.
- The condition can be transmitted when the parent feeds the chick.
- It can also be transferred from the parent to the egg,

- This is a hardy virus that can survive in the environment from about 6 months to 2 years.

Symptoms:
- Sudden feather loss
- Deformity in the feather
- Depression in the chicks
- Vomiting
- Lesions in the feathers
- Deformity or sudden degradation of the beak

Diagnosis
- Blood tests
- Feather biopsy
- Examination of the body post death

Prognosis
- In most cases the adults will be immune to the condition after being affected once. However, they may shed the virus or be carriers.
- Supportive care is the only option as there is no recommended treatment available.
- It usually results in the death of the infected bird, especially if they are young.

Polyomavirus

Transmission
- The virus can be transmitted through the feces, feather dander or by inhalation of virus present in the environment.
- It can be passed on from the hen to the chick.
- The virus is potent and can survive in the environment for several years.
- There are vaccinations available for newly hatched chicks.
- Chicks are most likely to be affected by the condition.

Symptoms:
- Weight loss

- Delayed emptying of the crop
- Anorexia
- Depression
- Vomiting
- Bleeding in the subcutaneous region
- Diarrhea

Diagnosis
- Blood tests
- Cloacal swab tests
- Necropsy or examination after the death of the bird.

Prognosis
- In case the chicks are infected, they will die in 48 hours.
- Adults may recover from the condition but will remain carriers most often.
- There is no specific treatment available.
- Supportive care is the best option to manage this condition.

Avian bornavirus

Transmission
- This is an enveloped virus that is less likely to survive outside the host.
- It is transmitted when birds come in contact with the contaminated body fluids, food or feces.
- The carriers of the condition will normally not show any symptoms of the condition.
- This is one of the least known diseases with no exact details on the incubation, prevalence and etiology.

Symptoms:
- Weight loss
- Impaired flight and balance
- Anorexia
- Depression
- Vomiting
- Wing flipping

- Abnormality in the movement of the head
- Toe tapping
- Motor deficit

Diagnosis
- Usually necropsy is the only option
- You will notice ganglia in the autonomic and peripheral nerves.
- Crop biopsy will reveal lesions.

Prognosis
- The bird will usually die in about 11 days of being infected or may survive for about 7 years with supportive care.
- There is no method of reliable treatment. Some medicines for the virus and the inflammation have been used experimentally.
- Good nutrition and quarantining measures will help you assist the bird in the recovery process.

Pacheco's disease

Transmission:
- This is a type of herpes virus that is transmitted through nasal and ocular discharge.
- The virus does not survive for long in the environment.
- Birds that are carriers will shed the virus that can only survive with a host.

Symptoms:
- Anorexia
- Diarrhea
- Sinusitis
- Diarrhea with blood
- Tremors
- Head tilting
- Seizures
- Excessive thirst
- Excessive urination
- Green or yellow droppings

Diagnosis
- Blood test
- Cloacal swab test
- Necropsy or examination after death

Prognosis
- Most birds will recover fully.
- Supportive care is the best option.
- There are a few recommended anti viral medicines that may be administered to the bird.

Psittacinepapillomatosis

Transmission
- This is also a type of herpes virus.
- Close contact with infection birds through feeding or when preening can lead to infection.

Symptoms:
- Lesions in the oral cavity
- Whitish, scaly warts in the mouth
- Lesions on the feet and toes
- Lesions in the cloaca
- Lesions on the eye or the eyelid
- Anorexia
- Vomiting
- Infertility
- Prolapse in the cloaca

Diagnosis
- A tissue that is affected by papillomatus will turn white when 5% acetic acid is added to it.
- Endoscopy
- Examination of lesions
- Necropsy

Prognosis
- The lesions must be removed surgically or with laser.

- If the GI tract is severely infected, it will lead to the bird's death.

You can consult your vet to stay updated in any developments in the treatment of the serious conditions. The more you learn, the more likely you are to spot the condition and look for timely assistance to help your bird.

3. Nutritional deficiencies in Caiques

One of the most important preventive measures to keep your bird healthy is to make sure that he has a balanced diet. Poor nutrition can lead to several health issues. Some of the most common problems that bird suffer from due to nutritional problems are:

Obesity

This condition is prevalent in many pet parrots. They are given a diet of high fat nuts, seeds and even table scraps. In some cases, overfeeding and not providing the bird with enough exercise will lead to obesity.

When a bird is about 20% more than the ideal weight, it is said to be obese. The weight of the bird's body will lead to lameness while he may experience respiratory issues if the concentration of the weight is in the abdominal area.

If your bird is diagnosed with obesity, it is a good idea to change the diet to a pelleted one with adequate portion control. Encourage your bird to exercise by keeping several food bowls around the cage to encourage him to walk around. Climbing and balancing toys also improve the physical activity of your bird.

Vitamin A deficiency

Vitamin A is one of the most important nutrients in a bird's diet as it affects the immune system. Seed diets that contain even 50% seed and 50% pellet lead to vitamin a deficiency or hypovitaminosis A.

The symptoms of vitamin A deficiency include:

- Sneezing
- Nasal discharge
- Periorbital swelling

- Conjunctivitis
- Dyspnea
- Excessive urination
- Excessive water consumption
- Blunt or absent papilla
- Anorexia
- Development of white plaques in the sinuses and eyes

The treatment process involves dealing with the secondary infections if any and supplementing the bird's diet with Vitamin A. You can add natural sources like spirolina to the food of the bird to get better results.

Iodine deficiency
Although this condition is not very prevalent with the fortified pet foods, you need to be aware that a deficiency of iodine can lead to goiter or thyroid hyperplasia.

The most common symptoms are:
- Wheezing
- Clicking
- Respiratory stidor

You can use Lugol's iodine until the signs of iodine deficiency have subsided or been removed completely.

Calcium, Vitamin D3, Phosphorous deficiency
Most seed based diets will lead to a deficiency in calcium, amino acids and phosphorous. These seeds are also quite high in their fat content.

Metabolic bone disease
If the bird has an unbalanced calcium to phosphorous ration, there are chances that he will develop hyperthyroidism. This is most common in younger and old birds.

Along with a lack of calcium, most birds have to cope with a deficiency in Vitamin D3 as they are housed indoors without adequate access to sunlight.

In case of younger birds, a lack of calcium in the diet will result in deformation and curvature in the longer bones as well as the vertebrae.

The common signs of metabolic bone disease are:
- Ataxia
- Seizures
- Deformation
- Repeated fractures
- Thin shelled eggs
- Decreased egg production and hatchability
- Death of the embryo
- Egg binding

The plasma calcium levels are studied to diagnose a possible deficiency in calcium levels. Supportive care along with necessary vitamin D and calcium supplementation is the best option. It is also a good idea to provide your birds with a full spectrum light if they do not have enough access to natural sunlight. In case of recurring fractures, bandaging and cage rest is necessary with adequate doses of pain killers.

If you can provide your bird with an outdoor cage, it will allow them to get natural light in abundance. If your bird's wings have been clipped, they can be taken outdoors provided you keep a close eye on them.

Vitamin D toxicosis
While excessive oral calcium does not cause any health issues in birds, if you give them too much oral vitamin D3, there could be an accumulation of calcium in the tissues of the body including the kidneys. Make sure that you provide supplements only after consulting the vet.

Iron storage disease
The condition of having excessive accumulation of iron in the liver is called iron storage disease. It is also called hemachromatosis. As the level of iron increases, the lysozomes in the liver get damaged and

release ions that lead to damage by oxidization in the membranes of the organs. It also leads to an improper metabolism of proteins.

Iron storage disease is not very common in pet birds but they are constantly at risk if proper diet is not provided. If the intake of iron is too high, it leads to this condition. There are other factors like genetic predisposition and stress that can cause this condition. Even an increased vitamin C intake will lead to storage of iron in the body.

The most commonly affected organs are the heart, liver and spleen.

The signs of iron storage disease include:
- Weight loss
- Depression
- Distended abdomen.
- Dyspnea
- Circulatory failure

The condition can be diagnosed with a biopsy of the liver. Treatment normally includes modification of the diet and removal of iron from the body. You must provide the bird with a lot of fiber to prevent accumulation of iron in the liver.

Other nutritional concerns
- A bird may develop sensitivity to certain preservatives and dyes present in pellets.

- They may experience a failure in the right side of the heart if the diet consists mainly of seeds.

- Improperly stored seeds will lead to cirrhosis.

- Your bird may not be eating everything that you provide even if you are making the effort of giving them a balanced meal. This must be dealt with by providing adequate supplements.

- If you are adding supplements make sure that the bird is observed properly. Usually, these supplements are not palatable and the bird may stop consuming water, leading to dehydration.

- Never give your bird any foods that contain caffeine, alcohol, salt, refined sugar or dairy products.

In the wild, Caiques spend most of their time foraging. In case of pet birds, they have access to one food bowl that gives them all their caloric intake. However with less energy spent, they will develop nutritional issues. Make sure that your bird has a healthy lifestyle.

It is a must to provide your bird with toys and adequate mental stimulation. A large enough cage is the first step to helping your bird burn some energy if it has enough toys and stimulators.

4. Caique first aid

Birds can have several injuries on a day-to-day basis and will need immediate and correct assistance. Make sure that you always have the emergency contact numbers handy and also a well maintained first aid kit to help your bird in time when it is needed.

The common injuries are:

- Broken wings or blood feathers: This may occur when you are trying to clip the feathers or due to the feathers getting stuck in toys etc. If the wing is broken, hold it close to the body and secure it with non-sticky tape or gauze. Make sure you don't tape it too tightly as it will cause breathing issues.

  If a blood feather breaks you will see lot of blood loss. You can just dab some styptic powder or flour on the area. Then, hold it down with some gauze and apply pressure to stop bleeding.

- Attack by a cat, dog or another bird: The first thing that you need to do is calm the bird down. You can place him in a separate cage in a quiet room. Then, examine the injuries. Bleeding can be stopped with styptic powder, flour and gauze. Treat a broken feather as mentioned above. The bird must be taken to a vet immediately as the saliva of a cat or dog can be toxic to birds.

- Abrasions and wounds: In the event that a bird comes in contact with a sharp surface, wounds may be caused. The first step is to clean the wound with hydrogen peroxide. Then take out any dirt or sharp objects using tweezers. You must also remove any feathers that are stuck on the wound. An antibiotic cream will help the wound heal. Make sure that your bird does not pick on the wound, as it will become deeper.

- Breathing issues: If you see strained breathing in your bird, check the nostrils for any foreign objects. Carefully remove the object using a pair of tweezers. Breathing with the mouth open indicates exhaustion or overheating. Outstretched wings mean that the bird needs to be cooled down instantly. That can be done by placing the bird in a dish of cold water or by holding a wet towel around his body. If you do not see blockage or heating, then the breathing issue is the result of an underlying illness that needs to be examined by a vet immediately.

- Burns: The area that is affected should be washed under running water immediately. You can then dab the area with gauze to dry it up. For mild burns, an ice pack will provide significant relief. If it is a major burn rush the bird to a vet. You must also take care to calm the bird down as a burn can lead to a lot of trauma.

- Chilling: If the bird is exposed to air conditioning or heavy drafts, it may lead to chilling. The body can be warmed up using a warm towel or a heat lamp. The temperature must be raised gradually. Overheating after chilling is quite common if the bird is under shock or if he has been injured. Thoroughly check the bird's environment for any chances of drafts. The best option is to relocate your bird's cage if you notice any issues.

- Toxication: The bird may come in physical contact with toxins or may inhale them. The most common sources of toxins are sprays, paint or even an AC vent. If the bird has ingested a toxin, it is a major cause for concern and you must call your vet immediately. You can even call any poison control authority in your area for immediate assistance. In this case, you will have to provide them with all details including the symptoms, the toxin the bird may have consumed and the amount of toxin consumed.

With timely assistance, most of these issues can be dealt with. The more observant you are of your bird, the faster you can provide him with the right first aid. You will also need to keep a few things handy to help your bird in time. Here is a list of items that you must have in your bird's first aid kit.

- An emergency contact number
- Number and directions to your vet's clinic
- A pair of tweezers
- Gauze roll to wrap the bird
- Antibiotic cream
- Hydrogen peroxide
- Thermometer
- A heating pad or lamp
- A large towel to hold the bird
- Syringe or a medicine dropper
- Gloves to keep your hands safe if the bird is not hand tamed yet.
- Scissors
- Q-tip for ointment application
- Sterilized gauze to manage bleeding
- Styptic pencil or flour

With these items in place you will not need to scramble and waste time when your bird does have an emergency. If you are leaving your bird under someone else's care, make sure you give them all the instructions required to take care of your bird in an emergency.

5. How to find a good vet
Caiques are exotic birds that need specialized care. You can consult a regular vet for any emergency. However, it is important for you to look for an avian vet who has experience working with exotic birds like Caiques. A good avian vet will be able to deal with specific health conditions that affect Caiques.

Finding a good vet requires you to do some research. Make sure you do this well before your bird comes home.

The first thing that you need to remember is that you need an Avian Vet who specializes in treating exotic birds. You should be able to find one located close to you after surfing the Internet. One of the most reliable sources of avian vet listings is the official website of the Association of Avian Vets or www.aav.org. They will list vets as per the locality and state.

Being associated with an avian vet who is affiliated with organizations like the AAV means that the vet is able to stay updated with the current trends in treating birds like Caiques, as these organizations have regular seminars and conferences that cover these subjects. There are a few things that you can ask your vet to confirm that your bird is in the right hands:

- How often do they treat birds? Ideally, the vet should be seeing at least 3 avian patients a day. If the number is about 3-4 a month, then the vet is not specialized in these birds. You can seek advice from them in an emergency but you will have to scout for someone with more experience in dealing with these birds.

- What are the methods that they use to keep themselves updated? You may not be able to ask them this question directly but you can certainly ask the vet if he or she is part of any avian vet group or you can ask about the last conference that he or she attended. You can even check for magazine or book subscriptions that the vet may recommend. This will tell you that he or she is genuinely working towards gathering as much information as possible when it comes to treating the bird.

- What are the types of parrots that they generally treat? This question will give you an idea about the variety of birds that the vet has experience with.

- How long does each examination take? Usually every bird will need a good 30 minutes. If the vet is only giving each bird about 10 minutes, then he may be overcrowded. While that speaks for the popularity of the vet, it does not really help your bird too much as sessions may be hurried.

- What are the emergency services provided? Is the clinic itself open for emergencies. In most cases, they will at least have affiliations with 24 hour services that will be able to attend to your bird in emergencies. Some vets are also available on call; which is certainly the ideal situation. However, they may be occupied with other cases at times and it is best if they are able to provide you with alternatives.

Walking around the clinic will also give you a fair idea about whether you are making the right choice or not. There must be basic amenities like a gram scale.

Observe how the vet handles the bird. If they are examining the bird in the cage, it may be an indication of inexperience unless there is any specific reason for keeping the bird inside the cage.

The staff should also be able to handle the bird comfortably. They must at least be able to identify the species of the bird that you have brought in. That is again an indication that there are avian patients who are often treated at the clinic.

You must also check the in-patient facilities. If they are admitting birds in the clinic after major procedures like surgeries, you will have to ensure that adequate quarantining methods are adopted to prevent any secondary infections in the birds that are admitted there.

Lastly, you must make sure that your vet is located at a convenient location. If not, every visit to the vet will end up being a stressful one for the bird. The vet must not be more than 15 minutes away from your home. This is also ideal when you do have an emergency.

In case your bird needs special care, your vet will be able to recommend the right facility. So, as long as the vet is competent to take care of the bird, it is better to look for a decent facility close to you in comparison to a high end one that is located far away.

You should also be able to build rapport with your vet. The way they handle your questions and whether they are interested in giving you information about the bird will tell you a lot about the personality of the vet. The vet will be an important part of raising your bird as you may have queries about your bird's health from time to time.

Once you have made the choice, ensure that everyone in your home has access to the contact details of the vet. They must also be provided to others who may care for your bird including pet sitters.

Chapter 8: Cost of Owning a Caique

Caique parrots are a big financial responsibility. This chapter will break down the cost of owning a bird. These costs are only the initial ones and may vary depending upon factors like the health of the bird, the number of toys you want to provide and lots more.

- Cost of the bird: $600 and upwards or £400 and upwards
- Cage: $600-1000 or £350-700
- Food and water bowls: $8-30 or £2-20
- Four to five toys: $20-100 or £10-75
- Perch: $6-15 or £3-10
- Ladder: $8-20 or £3-15
- Play stand: $30-200 or £15-100
- Cleaning supplies: $30 or £20
- One bag of bird food: £9-20 or £5-10
- Travel carrier: $25-80 or £10-50
- Veterinary exam (one)- $50-200 or £25-70

The total beginning supply costs will vary from $300-1200 or £150-700. This does not include variable costs like the cost of fresh produce. So, in totality, Caiques are a reasonably large financial responsibility and it is up to you to make sure that there are no compromises.

Conclusion

The world of Caiques is a very interesting one and you have hopefully been introduced to it through this book.

The fact that you have bought this book shows that you want to learn more about your pet bird or are trying to educate yourself about the bird before you bring one home. This indicates the makings of a very good Caique owner. You will certainly have a great bond with the bird you bring home.

Hopefully, the goal of helping you understand how much work you will have to put in when you raise a Caique has been fulfilled. If you still believe that you can manage a Caique, then you are in for several decades of unconditional companionship.

In your journey with your bird, try to educate yourself as much as you can about your bird. There is no end to how much you can learn. The more you know, the better you can make your bird's life.

Here is wishing you a fantastic time with your beautiful Caique bird.

Do leave us some reviews so that we can reach out to as many current and potential Caique owners as possible.

References

Staying updated about your bird's needs requires you to interact with other owners, learn from your vet and also do a lot of research on your own. There are several sources online that provide reliable information with respect to the health of your bird.

Note: at the time of printing, all the websites below were working. As the internet changes rapidly, some sites might no longer be live when you read this book. That is, of course, out of our control.

Here are some websites that you can visit to find reliable information about raising healthy and happy Caiques:

www.forums.avianavenue.com

www.birdtricks.com

www.caiquesite.com

www.shadypines.com

www.caiqueparrots.com

www.z13.invisionfree.com

www.beautyofbirds.com

www.adoptapet.com

www.betterwords.typepad.com

www.ccbirdclub.com

www.birds-at-home.blogspot.in

www.allpetbirds.com

www.goldencockatoo.com

www.petsuppliesplusfl.com

www.petcha.com

www.parrotforums.com

www.**parrot**debate.com

www.talkparrotlets.com

www.ur**parrot**.com

www.united**parrot**breeders.co.uk

www.findeen.co.uk

www.the**parrot**club.co.uk

www.precisely**parrots**.com

www.crazy**parrotforum**.myfast**forum**.org

www.**caiqu**ed.com

www.parrotchat.proboards.com

www.the**parrots**ocietyuk.org

www.tailfeathersnetwork.com

www.parrotwizard.com

26367448R00061

Printed in Great Britain
by Amazon